(G)race Equity

Reimagining Equity in the Workplace

(g)race·equity

Grace Equity is a challenge to our national dialogue about race. It calls upon all of us to shift our approach and perspectives of race/racism from fear, anger, and absolutism, toward humility, healing, and grace. This book was created to provide a pathway for organizations, activists, leaders, and race equity practitioners to be able to facilitate vulnerable and courageous conversations about racism and oppression, through the lens of grace.

Title: Grace Equity: Reimagining Equity in the Workplace
By: Dr. Michelle Majors
Edited by: 846 Global Publishing
Copyright 2022

DEDICATION

To My Sister
Nacala Mizan Ayele

So glad we chose each other for this lifetime.
Nailed it.

TABLE OF CONTENTS

INTRODUCTION 1

Chapter 1 - Leading with Grace 13

Chapter 2 – Truth and Reconciliation 27

Chapter 3 – Grace in The Public Square 35

Chapter 4 – Grace, Wokeness, and Cancel Culture......... 43

Chapter 5 – The Role of Grace and Race in the Nonprofit Space 53

Chapter 6 – Quiet Racism.. 73

Chapter 7 – Doing the Work...................................... 85

Chapter 8 – I am the Work 97

Chapter 9 – G.R.A.C.E. is.. 117

Chapter 10 - Bringing Grace to Organizational Conflict 127

Chapter 11 – We're All Swimmers 139

Works Cited 147

ABOUT THE AUTHOR... 149

INTRODUCTION

The global conversation about race has been intensifying throughout the 21st century. Though racism has always been a deep penetrating wound in our country, the connectivity of the internet has allowed more voices to be amplified worldwide and captures injustices in real time. This amplification has also given rise to a new level of evil and hatred that now sits at the forefront of our collective psyche. So, we watch in terror as shocking videos stun our national conscience and leave us despairing about how to fix it all. Pundits take to the airwaves to talk about how to calm race relations and build a more equitable society. But the drama continues to play out in governments, communities, schools, and organizations daily.

As I write this book, our country is reeling from its 232nd mass shooting this year. It is June. Many of these killings are racially motivated. In our classrooms, history that is deemed an unfavorable reflection of our American story is being stripped away. And the political divide is at an all-time wide. We seem, as a society, unable to agree on even the most basic ideals.

Mass shootings that are racially motivated leave communities asking tough questions that resist answers. The "why" question is chief among them. What were the forces, conditions, or circumstances that made such hate accessible, especially to someone so young?

In Buffalo, New York in 2022, a white man eighteen years old traveled three hours from his home to a supermarket in a predominantly Black neighborhood and unloaded 50 rounds on the shoppers there. When the smoke cleared, ten innocent lives were lost.

White Americans may likely never know what it means to read such a story and wonder how such hatred can rest in the human soul. It seems clear though, that the suspect harbored the deepest fear that white people are being replaced by Black people and other non-white, non-Christian citizens — enough that he was willing to kill.

Whenever these incidents occur, they leave an indelible mark on the hearts of Black people. "Could that have been my mother, sister, father, brother?" "Could that have been my son, daughter, aunt, uncle?" "Could that have been me?"

With psychological well-being assaulted once again, Black folks must go into the organizations where they work, serve, worship, and play, carrying the burden of every injustice leveled against the Black community and feeling as if the answers will never come.

Then, in those organizations, they must interact with people, trusting that they do not harbor similar feelings as the man who pulled the trigger. But they know the truth: racism speaks in many ways. For some, the sound of racism is the thundering crack of an assault rifle. For others, it is withholding vital information from people of color in an organization to ensure the white people in the organization maintain their advantage.

Despite all of our big talk about big ideas like "leveling the playing field," "diversity," "race equity," and "inclusivity," the reality of true racial equity seems to remain far out of our grasp. In fact, the more we discuss it, it seems, the more troubled our societies become. Beyond the headlines that draw attention to major injustice in the world, there are the millions of tiny clashes that break out which are so subtle, they aren't big enough to warrant a reporter and camera crew or make it on the national news circuit. But they are no less impactful to the people, more often people of color, that are harmed by these clashes. The tension and anxiety continue to grip our collective mind, body, and soul.

While our communities offer us insight into how poorly we fare bringing humanity together around issues of race, nowhere are the gaps between us more pronounced than in the workplace. The organizational climate is fascinating to study, because it is one of the few places where people are forced to interact with those who are not like them. People might choose to live in homogenous neighborhoods and socialize with people who come from the same ethnic group. But work environments don't afford those opportunities to escape the challenges of interacting with folks who look, dress, speak, think, and live differently.

As a result, the workplace can be rife with tension, and to navigate these tensions, people tend to learn how to become better and better at operating in stealth mode. You simply won't ever know what they really believe. Then there are the people who are fiercely loyal to their beliefs about race — and have no problems with anyone else knowing about them. And let's not forget those whose ideas shift with the cultural winds, doing whatever is in vogue in the racial landscape. To complicate matters, all of these people are supposed to find a "common ground", or "shared language."

Indeed, organizations are just as rocked by the tectonic plates of race relations that are always sliding beneath us. I engage with many organizations that are doing their best to steady the ground and create rails of stability. They institute policies that force us to "play nice" and "get along." They prescribe the language we should use to communicate with each other to demonstrate compliance. They bring in consultants like me with the hopes that we will "fix" them and show them the way.

Is any of this working? Clearly not.

All of these approaches are proven to be ineffective because of one primary issue – they only address one's *behavior* and not their *beliefs*. As a result, the workplace continues to be a place of great strife, confusion, resentment, and animosity. Many exhausted people of color continue to feel disenfranchised, unseen, unheard and thwarted in their attempts to rise in the ranks. They learn to modulate their tone, overlook the slights and insults, and keep pushing. They sit in implicit bias or microaggression trainings, frustrated that consultants have to come in to explain in *technical* terms, concepts that, for them, are so very experiential and visceral. Well-meaning white people stumble clumsily around trying to figure out ways to genuinely demonstrate their commitment to race equity. And of course, diehard separationists remain stalwart, using whatever power they have to keep their world under their control. And our quest for race equity continues.

This begs the questions, what are we missing?

Perhaps before we can talk about race equity, we must first turn to *grace. Grace equity.*

Grace Equity is a different way to engage in dialogue about race, racism, and injustice. It is a challenge to elevate organizational dialogue about race and explore something far more fundamental to the human experience – our desire to be seen and valued. It calls upon all of us to shift our approach and perspectives of race and racism away from fear, anger, and absolutism, toward humility, empathy, and compassion through the power of grace.

This is difficult and important work that few are willing to do. Grace requires those in power and privilege to let go of the control that they so depend on to keep them feeling safe. If grace is about

4

connection and empathy, and power is about control and access, then what is the motivation for those in power to lean into grace? And for those who have been harmed by historical, systemic, and social racism, grace just feels dangerous. Plain and simple. How do we bridge these gaps?

To make things more complex in an organizational context, people who have been historically excluded due to race are unfairly expected to guide and participate in the conversation about how to repair the organizational harms that they had no part in creating, and no institutional power to change. This is all while being asked to do so *with grace*. And yet, it happens. Time and time again, I see people of color come to the table with an earnest commitment to bring forth change in their organizations, without any institutional acknowledgment of the tremendous amount of grace and invisible labor that goes along with their efforts.

Racism is a system *designed* to be confusing and feel insurmountable. It keeps us divided and suspicious of one another. White leaders who earnestly want to make a difference and confront issues of racism within their organizations are often distrusted and held to a standard of impossible perfection in their efforts. Mostly by other white staff members, but also staff of color. Any mistakes they make are often seen as a validation of their racial incompetence at best, and racism at worst. Leaders of color are under the pressure to prove their worthiness as leaders, while, at the same time, soothing and reassuring their teams past their internalized fears and biases that are often masked as organizational concerns and wellbeing.

One byproduct of historical and systemic racism is that it leads us to turn away from our highest instincts as human beings. Things that we would instinctively do, we second-guess and question when the dynamic of race is layered in.

In season three, episode four of the hit TV show, *Blackish*, the main character, Dre, is shown entering his place of work one morning. When the elevator door opens, he sees a cute three-year-old white girl standing in the elevator unattended. Of course, most of us would assume she was lost. We would spring to action, helping the little girl find the adult she was separated from. However, in the scene, Dre looks around suspiciously as if a trap has been set for him, and slowly backs away from the elevator as the doors close with the little girl still inside.

The scene then cuts to his two white colleagues reviewing the security tape of Dre leaving the little girl in the elevator. They are lambasting him for his heartlessness. They are outraged that Dre didn't help her. Dre begins to explain to them that as a Black man, he is typically seen as a threat. As a Black man he is assumed guilty and must prove himself innocent. It could be dangerous for him to be found with a little white girl. As Dre continues his explanation, his Black colleague, Charlie comes in and says, "I'm sorry I'm late, there was a little white girl in the elevator, so I had to take the stairs." Soon after, another Black male colleague, Curtis comes in apologizing for being late, stating, "There was a little white girl in the elevator, I saw my freedom flash before my eyes."

As the saying goes, "many a true thing is spoken in jest."

The implication here is what many Black folks know; there is a history of Black men being taken to jail or killed for the mere perception of being too comfortable with white girls and women. Black folks know that when it comes to us, law enforcement will shoot first, convict first, or execute first. Then they'll ask questions later. So, it behooves us to walk away rather than take the chance of losing our lives or freedom.

This is what racism does. It overrides that highest part of ourselves. It has us second guess our most basic instinct of humanity,

6

connection and helping one another. I mean, who wouldn't help a three-year-old child who appears to be lost?

Grace must be available to all of us in the process of healing the racial divide: leaders and workers, victims and perpetrators, confessors, and forgivers. That is why the time for this conversation about grace is timely or, perhaps, long overdue.

When you hear the word "grace," what do you think of? Some of you may immediately wander to the religious or spiritual themes of your childhood or lived experience. I believe that grace lies at the heart of many religions, but this book is not a religious discussion of grace. While this book explores the inner workings of human interaction in the organizational setting, it also contextualizes grace as an inner revelation and transcendent awakening as well as an outward expression. Grace is a powerful force that can transform the landscape of the workplace in lasting and meaningful ways and bridge the gap from one person to the next in ways rules and mandates never could. To this end, I suppose one could perceive grace in a spiritual or religious context.

In boardrooms all across the world, a dozen or more people sit around a table attempting to coalesce around a particular goal, mission, or objective. Frankly, it is a nearly impossible task. It is a miracle that humanity is able to collaborate at all, regardless of race. We are so diverse in ways that have nothing to do with the color of our skin or the culture that produced us.

Gather any twelve people from any organization and you must acknowledge that those twelve individuals bring with them a dozen backgrounds, attitudes, mindsets, habits, fears, hopes, and prejudices. Regardless of race, we all have them. Some people are organized; others are messy. Some are measured; others are risk-takers. Some are visionaries and creatives; others are grounded implementers and task masters. Add race to the mix along with the social norms and customs that accompany how people interact, and it is a wonder we get anything done at all.

But somehow, we do. Somehow, we can move past these differences and achieve amazing things together.

When it comes to the issue of race, grace is in short supply. Especially in the workplace. We all come to the discussion of race with different perspectives and lived experiences. Whether we are people of color who have been harmed by the weapon of racism or white people who have been beneficiaries of it, we arrive with our tensions locked in place. It is my hope that, through the work we will do together in the coming chapters, we can see each other, *truly see each other,* through the lens of grace, in ways we may not have ever seen each other before.

Now, before we start, let me be clear. This book is not for people at the extremes of the racial conversation. White supremacists, nationalists, and terrorists are unable and unwilling to process the complexities and healing power of grace. Breaking through the walls they have erected is a lifelong venture and this book offers them nothing toward that end.

Secondly, it must be noted that many folks of color, especially Black and Indigenous people, understandably struggle with this idea of race/racism within the context of grace when we have experienced so much hate, abuse, and systemic torture over the centuries. However, just like white Abolitionists in the 1800's, or white Freedom Riders during the Civil Rights Movement, there are many white people who *are* allies, who *are* in the fight with us, and freedom for all requires all of us to engage. It requires a trust that only grace can create. So, for everyone reading this book please know that for people of color, especially Black and Indigenous folks, it takes not only grace for us to continuously show up to this work, but an irrational faith to believe that anything can ever come from our doing so.

For those people of color who choose not to participate in this work, I ask that we give them the grace of *acceptance and self-care*. Some folks of color are just too exhausted from this work. Let them be.

Thirdly, many will express concern that white people may weaponize the idea of grace so that they don't have to be accountable for the things they do, say, and think. They may use grace to lighten the blow when they make a mistake. Instead of owning what they did, they will ask for grace for what they did. Or they may use the grace extended to them as justification to continue to inflict intentional harm. This is one of the inevitable downsides of grace. If people are going to cause harm, any reason will suffice to rationalize it. Just like a hammer can be used to build or tear down, some will use grace to further injure.

But even in that circumstance, grace has a role to play. We should never discount the impact that grace can have on even the hardest of hearts. If enough of us are working on the side of good, the cause of grace equity is advanced. Detractors will either have to join or move out of the way.

Fourth, as I write about grace, I am angry, hurt, sad, and fearful about what people who look like me face every day in this country. Often, I question my own faith and ability to tap into grace. Recently, my husband and I watched the Netflix series, *Monster: The Jeffrey Dahmer Story*. [Content Warning: Graphic] The story was about serial killer Jeffrey Dahmer and his heinous murders, necrophilia, and cannibalism of 17 men (and boys) of color who identified as gay. However, I was fixated on how many of those murders could have been avoided if they had listened to Dahmer's neighbor, Glenda, who called the police numerous times over several months to express her concern about the bumping, screaming, drilling, and odor coming from Dahmer's apartment next door. Glenda was a Black woman. No one believed her or took her seriously enough to come and check things out. Every time Glenda engaged with the police, and was subsequently ignored, I felt the same intense rage, and overwhelming hopelessness that she portrayed. This movie should have been titled *"That Time When Ten Men and Boys Died in Apartment 213 Because No One Ever Believes Black Women."* So again, I hurt. I am often afraid. I am angry too. But what I know for sure is that we can't force, shame, or train our way out of this mess that we are in. I am proposing we try compassion, humanity, and grace.

Finally, grace is not about accepting abuse from anyone. I will talk about grace as a model between people who have the same baseline of humanity. When dealing with a narcissist or sociopath, grace only fuels their manipulation. In some cases, the grace to give is to yourself. This work requires discernment. Grace is a gift to give, and some aren't worthy of that gift.

Grace Equity in organizations cannot solely be a top-down approach with mandates from managers and CEOs to the masses who work for them. If it is, it will be forced, awkward, and insincere. At the same time, however, it cannot be solely a bottom-up approach. If it is, it will be thwarted, choked, poisoned, and derailed by unfavorable policies and toxic cultures that never allow it to flow fast and free.

Grace that is forced by anyone — bosses, employees, governments, parents — lacks authenticity and doesn't have staying power. But grace extended willingly to others in any relationship is infectious. It permeates the heart, mind, and soul, bringing healing to broken places. It weakens prejudice and discrimination. It saturates the atmosphere with cooperation and shapes cooperative cultures. It dilutes judgment and criticism. And it creates the much-needed path to the race equity so many of us long to see.

Everyone wins. Collaboration and teamwork are enhanced. The job satisfaction of each individual employee improves. And the valuable knowledge we gain about equity has ripple effects far beyond the hours of 9 to 5 as we wield the tools to learn, grow, and talk about race in a way that creates vulnerability and connection, rather than division and pain.

CHAPTER 1 – LEADING WITH GRACE

I believe one of the most overlooked but effective leadership qualities is grace. This is a powerful way for leaders to connect with the minds and hearts of their teams. Grace is a style of leadership that is centered on authentic caring and commitment toward the success of the organization and the people in it. There is a certain confidence that is quiet, yet absolute. There is an elegance in how grace leaders humanize, and bring out the best in their teams. They are nuanced, yet boldly explicit in word and deed. But above all, they are clear about who they are. Even when they don't know exactly what to do, they are confident enough to say so and humble enough to seek help from their trusted team. When they make mistakes, they admit them and are often met with grace and forgiveness by their teams, because the leader has demonstrated safety, authenticity, and humanity that allows others to see themselves in the situation.

These kinds of leaders are far more effective in their organizational race equity efforts because of the volatility and likelihood for making mistakes that comes along with doing this work. Showing your humanity and vulnerability upfront goes a long way in how your team responds to your mistakes. Other leaders who have built their identity on knowing it all or looking good greatly struggle in this work. There are simply too many conflicting dynamics that can arise that require humility and vulnerability.

For example, in 2020, during the height of the George Floyd protests, I had a client that received a large sum of money from a philanthropist to help figure out what would be the best use of a very large financial investment toward Black men in our country. It would be a game-changing amount of money for millions of Black men in our country. This project involved a researcher to pull the data together and consultants to help facilitate the process, and my client would be the voice of the project, essentially doing the framing and marketing.

One day, some of the team members reached out to me with a significant equity issue. They were upset that, while this project was in service of helping Black men, there was not a single Black man as part of the process. The researcher, consultants, my client, the philanthropist, none were Black. The organization's Equity Team was incensed. And the Director, I'll call him Bill, was committed to the financial gains of this contract with this philanthropist, hoping that it can open the door to other contracts.

The Equity Team felt tokenized, infantilized, and angry that this kind of situation was exactly why they were created, yet their concerns weren't being heard. They believed that this was a moment for organizational reflection to address inequitable outcomes that result from people of color being excluded from processes that specifically concern them.

They also felt this situation was specifically racialized as one stated, "If this was an investment into women's reproductive rights, I am confident that people would see how weird it would be not to have any women in the process."

Bill, on the other hand, couldn't see how his staff didn't understand that this was a financial decision that would impact his ability to "keep the lights on." For him, it wasn't an option. Also, this process was all happening in a six-week window of time. So, there would be no time to change course, and he simply wasn't going to walk away from the opportunity.

In a last-ditch effort to appease staff, Bill reached out to the community and "found" Black men to participate in the process as a community panel. This only infuriated staff more because, "Now we are dealing with absolute tokenism in its most fundamental sense of the word," said one staff member.

In the end, Bill moved forward with this client and the Black men on the "panel." This sank staff morale and the Equity Team soon disbanded. Had he been leading with grace, Bill would have brought the opportunity to the team before the decision was made. He would have been dialed into his team enough to know that this would be a sticking point for them and to get ahead of it through transparency, dialogue, and authentic sharing about his financial concerns and the opportunity that this client presented. With all of this he could have moved to a place of collaboration and inspiration such that his team felt heard and seen, even if they had landed on the same decision to move forward with the client.

What grace leaders know is that it's often more about the voices that are part of the process than the choices made at the end of the process that are most important.

One thing about Bill that wasn't explicitly stated in this story was that he had an enormous ego, and all of his staff knew and felt it. The byproduct of a leader with a huge ego is:

1. **A culture of toxic positivity.** This was an organization where "everything is great," and if you have a complaint or concern, make sure to bring a solution with it. And make sure you frame your concern not as a complaint but an exciting opportunity for growth. Ego is a huge barrier to grace.
2. **The inability to hear critical feedback.** As it happened, when I interviewed all his staff and gave him their feedback, he told me essentially that they were lying, they

misunderstood him, or they were the ones that were fragile. Not in those exact words, of course. But essentially so. When I explained to him that some of his staff was afraid to share their ideas with him especially if they were contrary to his ideas, he replied, "I think that the people who don't speak up are people who lack confidence and wouldn't have spoken up anyway."

3. **Cluelessness about privilege and staff needs.** As a reward for a job well done, he once gave a particular team the gift of an overnight stay at his golf club. While reserving their rooms, they learned that not only did this club not allow children, but there was a two-night minimum, and they were expected to pay for the additional night.

To be clear, Bill hired me because he was genuinely committed to bringing DEI principles to his organization. He just didn't realize what the cost would be to make the adjustments that needed to be made. Of course, I am not speaking of financial costs, but the cost to his identity. The changes he would need to make as a leader. The truths that he'd have to admit to himself. I was clear that the price was too high for this leader to pay. My time soon ended.

Using Bill as an example, we will unpack the three aspects of leadership that I talk about in my book, "Trust the Process."

Leadership of Self

Bill wasn't aware of how he was showing up and because he was in denial, he couldn't do the necessary inner work to grow.

Grace is a leadership style that can be learned and developed, but it can't be faked. People will see right through it in the moment of stress when we revert right back to our basic instincts and tendencies. What makes this leadership style tricky is that it only works when you are being authentic and relaxed *within yourself*.

Many of us have no clue who we are in general, and this spills into our leadership. You must know who you are in order to know who you are *as a leader*.

For example, I grew up in conditions of chronic homelessness. This is when I very viscerally understood voicelessness. I was at the mercy of whoever we lived with. I had to learn and adopt their values, beliefs, habits, and idiosyncrasies. I couldn't get mad or sad because I couldn't afford to disrupt their home, and our shelter, with futile things like my emotions.

One time we lived with a white woman and her daughter Kenna. Kenna was a nasty hell-brat who took every opportunity to tease and humiliate my sister who was of the same age as Kenna. She would flaunt candy, cookies, new clothes, whatever it was, in front of my sister. I wanted to beat her down so bad. I remember my throat would burn from all the choking back the anger and rage I felt for her, and my mother for putting us into this situation. One day, Kenna had some cookies and asked my sister if she wanted one. When my sister said yes, Kenna replied, "Ok, then bark like a dog." I ran into the room just as Kenna was throwing the cookie across the room telling my sister to "fetch it". Did I mention how badly I wanted to beat this 10-year-old girl down? The odd thing is that I remember being angry at my sister for saying "yes". In retrospect, I realize that I got mad at her because I didn't have permission to be mad at anyone else. This is also when I learned to never ask for anything from anyone, AND never accept help when offered.

I couldn't wait to become an adult so that I never had to put up with the Kennas of the world. I never had to do whatever people wanted me to do. I could do things on my own and for myself. Fast forward to adulthood. The minute I feel micromanaged, or that I'm being forced to do something, I get anxious, resistant, and what seems to be irrationally angry because it reaches those pain points of the unhealed wounds from my history. In reaction to the unhealed wounds of that experience, I became someone who absolutely must have my own agency, voice, and choice, because I had none of these as a young person.

On the flipside, this experience has led to one of my greatest strengths. My ability to read the room and read people. Having to live with different people, I quickly learned to understand what people value. I learned to hear what was not said. I learned to be tuned in to the frequency of what people were feeling. I learned to move on instinct, or what seems to make the most sense rather than external data. All these gifts were developed as a matter of survival but became the keys to my success as a consultant, trainer, facilitator and coach.

I know what it's like to be unseen and dismissed. When you don't have a place to live domestically, it's hard to find a place to live psychologically and spiritually. Going in and out of social service agencies where the service workers routinely disregard your humanity and dignity, it's easy to feel like you don't matter.

This experience has led me to be a people-first leader and a good listener. My number one priority is to ensure that people who talk to me and work with me feel seen and heard. For that reason, I must have freedom to make my own choices and come and go as I please. I'm super selective with clients, because if I don't feel right about them, I can't work with them.

What I can say for sure is that I know, accept, and love who I am and who I'm not, always growing and evolving. So as a leader, I can be authentic, relaxed, and free when I walk into spaces. I'm ok with people not liking me or my style. This comes in handy when I fall on my face—which happens a lot in this work.

We read books, and learn techniques, but miss the most important part of inner reflection that lies at the heart of this work. I have given leaders tools for communication, tools for goal setting, and tools for conflict resolution. But, if a "leader" can't own his or her mistakes, be vulnerable, own strengths and weaknesses, speak from the heart with grace and transparency, these tools are useless.

The ability to be authentic and free becomes invaluable when dealing with matters of racism, since racism brings up our insecurities, fears, and anxiety. Racism brings out the worst in us. If you don't have access to your truest authentic self, you will act and do what you "think" you should be doing, instead of what you "know" is the right thing to do.

Brace yourself; here comes the woo-woo part. You must do your work to know yourself. Do you accept yourself? Love yourself? Instead of being imprisoned by playing the role of a leader, you can be free to be a leader.

Leadership of Others

Bill didn't trust his team; therefore, he wasn't honest with them. He wasn't truly collaborative, and he couldn't tap into the strengths and genius of his staff through the power of grace.

In full disclosure, I will acknowledge that at the start of the writing of this book, the world is positioned on the backside of a global pandemic that turned our lives upside down. Many would argue that grace has been extended as a matter of survival in business. People had to arrive at work late and leave early. People had to pick up slack for others who had to care for loved ones, or themselves. The toll on our mental health, personal lives, and overall performance has been enormous. The question for us now is whether or not we will continue to lead our teams with this kind of grace as a standard practice?

The nature of grace is quite unique from the many other virtues we espouse as human beings. Grace, though sweet in sound, is a bitter pill to swallow as leaders because it inherently includes traits we do not typically value in business, nor in daily life. My belief about grace is that it is:

- Undeserved
- Unconditional
- Unilateral
- Protective
- Forgiving
- Safe

Let's unpack each one.

Grace is undeserved. A person can do absolutely nothing to *earn* grace. It does not require a request from the potential receiver. Instead, it is freely offered from one person to another or from a person to an organization, or from one leader to their team. It makes allowances for mistakes and gives the receiver the time to right their wrongs. And, since it cannot be earned, it is always extended at the discretion of the giver.

Grace is unconditional. It is not based on any set of criteria upon the receiver. There are no strings attached. As such, grace should not be negotiated. Instead, it should be freeing, as we will discuss in a moment.

Grace is unilateral. While two people can offer each other grace, the grace can only be given by one person to another. It flows in one direction only. Each one makes the decision to extend grace without expecting or requiring anything in return.

20

Grace offers a level of protection. Grace makes a promise that the wrongdoing is under its umbrella of protection. It cancels debts and absolves past guilt as it looks forward to ensuring past harms are not repeated.

Grace is forgiving. Grace allows for forgiveness to take place. The future cannot be secured if the weight of past harm bears heavy on the guilty party. Grace allows an organization to acknowledge the past and then mark a new starting line from which a better outcome is possible. Grace allows leaders to make mistakes and restore those harmed.

Grace is safe. Grace creates true safe spaces because it allows people to be vulnerable, understanding that they will not be harmed for sharing their hearts. That is why true apologies often flow in spaces where grace is abundant. It sets an environment where guards can be lowered, and real dialogue can occur that might lead to reconciliation.

Perhaps now you see why grace is a tough order to fill, and one of the reasons we often associate grace with God and religion. It can feel like acts reserved for the supernatural.

However, there is a way to bring this very divine act to the realm of mere mortals. And the key to this sacred space is empathy. When the word empathy was coined, as far as etymologists can tell, it was used by German psychologists to suggest a method of "feeling in," or "acting as if" (Lanzoni, 2015) Psychologists would have their patients literally take on the persona of the person they were learning to have empathy for. By pretending to be the person, the patient was more able to feel what it must be like to be them. The doctors wanted their patients to not just recognize what those feelings might be, but to actually experience the sadness, grief, pain, anger, or other emotions that person might have felt or might continue to feel. That is the "feeling in" the doctors were after — and the kind of empathy we are seeking when we propose grace equity.

I believe that one of the biggest factors in the perpetuation of racism is people's inability to feel what it must be like to be other than who they are at present. If a white man knew what it was truly like to be a Black man, he would understand the Black man's fear of police. Conversely, if people of color knew what it was like to be a white person who walks on the tightrope of allyship, people of color might better understand a white person's frustration, guilt, and missteps. As a white person that is truly committed to equity and justice for all, there comes the navigation of all the moving dynamics of allyship. If I say or help too much, I'm a savior. If I don't say enough then I'm silent and complicit. If I say too much I'm taking up too much space. If I say it the wrong way or in a way that is misunderstood, I'm deemed a racist. All of this is real. Racism affects so many of us, but because we are sitting in our own pain and perspective; it's hard for us to connect and understand one another. And that is where grace comes in.

3. Leadership in systems and organizations

When we can identify policies that are clearly fraught with racist undertones, we must summon the courage to call them out and commit to solutions. This is never easy because racist mindsets tend to view a complaining person of color as a "troublemaker" or "angry," especially if they are Black. These are monikers no one wants to wear. Many of us have seen images of the smiling slave. Despite their torturous life, the slave was expected to always smile so that their captors would not feel threatened, afraid, or disrespected. But it is necessary to take the risk to bring attention to the systemic forces that keep racism alive and well. Remaining silent only allows the system to grow in strength and affect new generations.

Racial healing in organizations must spring from the healing power of grace if we are to dismantle the system of white supremacy within. Only grace will provide the space for what needs to be said and done to undo the traumas and wounds inflicted on people of color from historically racist and harmful practices that work to keep them disenfranchised. And grace is required for those who must do the difficult work of reversing the tide since racism is not just an issue for people of color, it's an issue for us all. However, it is the burden of the white community to purge racism from the systems they have purposely or involuntarily benefitted from all their lives.

Getting back to empathy, if people are allowing themselves to feel the way others in the organization feel, what happens when they have to confront the unpleasant emotions that might reside in an organization or in the people involved?

Often, initial discussions about equity, inclusion, and diversity are done with the help of a facilitator or a team of facilitators. The facilitator or committee often has the power to judge when a statement being offered in equity discussions crosses the line, moving from expressions of true self-awareness to racist comments that don't move the conversation forward.

That said, people on all sides of the equity discussion must be prepared to hear the other. In elevating collective thinking and understanding of racism and its impact on individuals within the organization, it can sometimes require conversations that are difficult to engage in. But when grace is centered, it's possible.

We must study the big picture systems and structures in our organizations to determine how they have supported discrimination against people of color. This can often feel like eating an elephant, since there are so many places where racism has taken root. Dissecting the organization into smaller parts in light of the larger organizational context is a more manageable approach. Then we can see how smaller actions affect the bigger vision.

As organizations evaluate themselves through the lens of grace, I suggest focusing on the following four key areas and asking the reflection questions that I discuss in my book, *Trust the Process*. You can see those four areas and reflections questions in the chart below:

Focus Area	Reflection Questions
Office Culture	• Are there clear stated values or community norms on how we speak to and treat one another? • Do we implicitly or explicitly indicate that some people or roles are valued over others? For example, attorneys over support staff? Staff with longer tenure over new staff. • Do we have practices of celebration and acknowledgments of staff? • Do we have informal opportunities to talk about race such as book clubs, lunch and learns, shared experiences and reflections? • Is our staff free and open to disagree, question, or dissent? • Do we have a culture that values work life balance and does leadership model that? Does leadership send emails at 3am? Do they call in while on vacation? • What other things do we **say** we value and then **do** the opposite? • Are there known problematic individuals who say or do offensive things that people complain about, but they are never reprimanded? • Do we have a culture of rushing from fire to fire, or do we have time to plan and create, and handle crises with deliberation and thoughtfulness? • When there are non-mandatory social activities does most of the staff attend?

	• Do we engage and ask staff what they need or do we assume and act on behalf of staff without collaboration?
Leadership Development Opportunities	• Do we have or need a mentorship program? • Do we have a formal process for leadership/ professional development and promotions? • Do all staff know how to access and engage in this process? • Do all managers provide their teams with the option to engage in this process? • What other ways can we support the team in their growth and development? • Do we have a high turnover of people of color or people from other marginalized identities? If so, can we identify any of the factors they had in common? i.e., common manager, department, identity, branch location, length of employment, etc.?
Hiring Practices	• Does the job description allow for lived experience, or is more valued based on formal education or professional experience? Is this what we want? • Is our salary or salary range listed? • Are we posting our jobs in places that ensure we can have a diverse pool of candidates? • Do we articulate our commitment to diversity in our description? • Do we require staff to have a baseline of professional and/or lived experience in the area of diversity and equity? • Is there a standardized hiring process that includes a broad swath of representation i.e., ethnic, hierarchical, gender, length of tenure, etc. • Do we have training or written documentation that helps panel members identify, name, or check their biases, so that there can be group support in mitigating bias. • What is the process for selection? Is there a clear understanding about who makes the final decision? • What are the contingencies *in writing* if the hiring panel and final decision maker (typically director) disagree on candidates? • Is there a consistent formal orientation that ensures that everyone who is hired understands our organizations commitment to equity and what to do

	if you experience something that you feel may be racial or equity related? • Once a candidate is selected, how is the interview panel acknowledged? All staff email? Time off? Gift card?
Problem-Solving of Employee Concerns	• Is the process for managing staff conflict clear and accessible? • Is it consistent for all staff, regardless of position, tenure, race, gender, etc.? • Is the HR team on staff trained on the nuance and dynamics regarding racism? Bias? Microaggressions? Are they able to facilitate dialogue between individuals of different racial identities when an issue of race or racism arises? If not, should we hire an equity director or role that is trained in this kind of situation? • Do we have a conflict resolution process that is restorative or punitive? • Can staff in conflict choose to opt into a restorative justice process where they can try to work out differences in a space of grace? If so, do you want to consider that as a viable conflict resolution model?

To understand, access, and extend grace, we must accept its nature. Grace propels us from our comfort zones into a place that is unfamiliar and, perhaps, awkward. That is where policies and procedures (as well as in-depth conversations) can help us bridge the gap from ignorance to truth, oppression to equity, and race equity to grace equity.

CHAPTER 2 – TRUTH AND RECONCILIATION

"You can't heal what you won't reveal."

The sight of South African Bishop Desmond Tutu crumbling in his seat, resting his head on the table in front of him and shaking as he sobbed is an image that anyone who has seen, will not soon forget.

The year was 1995, and the descriptions of horror shared with the Truth and Reconciliation Commission, led by Tutu, are almost too horrifying to repeat. The commission had been established for one major purpose: to systematically repair the harm caused by Apartheid from 1960 to 1994. As he listened to people share their stories on the first day, he sat stoically — almost expressionless. But he was unable to maintain his composure. After just two days of hearings, his fortitude gave way and the floodgates opened as he listened to the cries of the abused, victimized, and disenfranchised. Their sufferings conveyed horrors that no human heart should ever know.

"Don't you remember torturing me?" one man asked his torturer (Facing History and Ourselves, 2010).

"What kind of man are you that would do this to another human beings?", ask another man to the same torturer (Facing History and Ourselves, 2010)

The commission investigated thousands of gross human rights violations that were perpetuated during Apartheid. Upon its conclusion, only a few trials were held for the most heinous crimes. But more importantly this commission allowed the South African people and the world to hear what the victims had to say — to give the victims a safe forum to release the horrors locked up in their souls. It was also a time for some of the perpetrators of the terror to speak as they confronted their own guilt and shame. No apologies were demanded though many were offered. This was not about forgiving the past, which was decidedly unforgivable. This commission was seeking to carve out a path forward together between the oppressors, and those they had subjugated for decades.

Truth and reconciliation are powerful words when applied to any human interaction. Whether it's spouse to spouse, friend to friend, parent to child, perpetrator to victim, or organization to employees — we require truth if we are going to experience reconciliation. Lies are a natural barrier to grace.

Truth

We often describe truth as light, and accurately so. But light does not always have the same effect in every situation. We pretend as if light is always dialed up slowly like a gentle sunrise, growing and growing until it shines its warm radiance through a glass-paned window. But imagine the effects of light if you have been in a dark cave. Then, light is jolting — painful, even. It causes you to squint your eyes and shield them from the brightness. You turn your head and cover your face. In the same way light can warm a chilly morning, it can also burn like a laser, ripping anything in its path in two.

Organizations, particularly in America, desperately need light. But, sadly, many of them remain in a deep dark cave. How does one shine the light of truth on them without blinding them? How can we warm with the light of truth, stopping short of disintegrating those at whom it is aimed?

And, what if the truth is unclear, contested, or hard to hear? What if truth sparks anger and outrage? And what if truth leaves people on opposite sides of a chasm so wide, there seems to be no bridge long enough to connect them?

First, telling the truth can have serious implications in an organization, especially if it requires acknowledging things that could open the door to legal actions by former or current employees. Telling the truth could require the removal of certain staff. It will likely dismantle long standing policies. Of course, these are all things to be considered. But there is always a way to both tell the truth while protecting the organization. I had a former client who had this very concern. Their legal counsel advised the Executive Director to refrain from using the word "harm" and instead use the word "impact."

Another thing about truth telling is that, more often than not, those who benefit from lies will have a difficult time relinquishing the power or advantages that they have enjoyed. I see this often when working with organizations that have staff members who have been there for decades and who seem to be struggling with these new concepts of equity, diversity, and inclusion.

> *There's my truth, your truth, and THE truth. It seems that most of our biggest problems stem from fighting for our truth as if it is THE truth.*

When you open Pandora's box and let the truth fly free, you take a risk. After all, one person's truth often does not match another's, and there is disagreement about what the truth really is. And, in the best of circumstances where everyone agrees about what happened, the truth can be difficult to discuss. Not to mention, what do we do with the realities released from the mystic Pandora's box? They must be reconciled, or they become torturous.

Therefore, it is important to have a process where one's truth is not up for debate. The nature of a truth and reconciliation process like the one South Africa instituted is for everyone to have their own voices and share their own experiences. Otherwise, people debate truth as a defense mechanism to protect their job security, personal identity, or privileges, as opposed to focusing on healing and restoration.

That was Nelson Mandela's goal and the reason there was no punishment for most of those who confessed. Though Mandela is widely regarded as a hero, not everyone agreed with how he managed power when it passed to him after the fall of apartheid. Many, frankly, wanted blood. They wanted him to redress the crimes of the former decades of pain and suffering with the blood of the oppressors.

But Mandela refused to respond to oppression with oppression. Instead, he sat down with the most vile and disreputable among the apartheid regime and offered the last thing they expected to receive: grace.

Mandela recognized that the system was the problem, not the people. This is a tougher leap to make than you might imagine. After all, you can't talk to "the system" or look it in the eye. You can't reason with the system or shake it by its shoulders and ask it what it was thinking when it did what it did. It can feel rather benign to fight an enemy you can't see. It's far easier to look at the person who committed the act of aggression, suppression, racism, discrimination, etc. and point a self-righteous finger at them, demanding apologies, retribution, and restitution.

Imagine what it might look like if the United States of America conducted its own Truth and Reconciliation Commission that was tasked with identifying and publicly acknowledging past harms and abuse and committed by our government; with the aim of healing and restoration both those who have been harmed, as well as those who did the harming?

More than 50 countries have undergone such a process (Wikipedia, 2022). The Australian government created a commission to address the violence against Aboriginal people during colonization. Canada created a commission to address the human rights abuses and murders in the Canadian Indian Residential School System. Rwanda created a Commission for national healing after the Rwandan Genocide. The list goes on.

And yet, in the United States, a country that is regarded as one of the most sophisticated, wealthy, free, and advanced nations in the world, the concept of a formal reconciliation process hasn't been considered as a viable means of moving us forward to heal our ever-widening racial divide.

I honestly believe this is because the truth would rock this country to its core.

When we begin to truly see each other's humanity, which a truth and reconciliation process would allow, we will become unified. People would begin to figure out that it's not each other that we should focus on, it's the system. The system that we inherited. The system that depends and thrives on our division and hatred.

Our system was not designed for collective care, action, healing, compassion, joy, and peace. Division, hate, and competition are what keep our motor running. The idea of being "better than them" fuels that motor. What would happen if we all agreed to lay down our literal and metaphorical weapons and just mind our own business and seek our highest joy? Who would we be if we weren't fighting and trying to prove ourselves?

How many people would quit their jobs? How many people would start new businesses contributing innovative ideas to our marketplace? How many would be able to get off their antidepressant and anxiety medications now that they are free to be whoever they want to be? I am clear that there are many reasons that people use mental health medication. I do believe that many issues stem from feeling trapped and stuck in the cycle or proving themselves, or having to be someone they don't want to be.

Reconciliation

What people faced in apartheid with its government sanctioned murders, death squads, rapes, and imprisonments; or what American slaves endured with the whippings, hangings, separation from families, and subjugation of mind, heart, body, and spirit does not compare to what happens in organizational settings today. Getting overlooked for a promotion or being gaslit by colleagues or harassed due to the color of your skin is hardly the same as being enslaved or killed. But it rises from the same toxic and cancerous mindset. And it produces the same kind of frustration, anger, and fear. It may not kill the body, but it can destroy the spirit.

So, what does reconciliation mean in a grace space?

I'll start off with a 2003 article by Laura Davis. Davis shares four types of reconciliation. The four bullets below can be found at psychotherapynetworker.com:

1. **Deep mutual healing.** This first is the one we long for the most in which both people grow and change, and there is a deep healing in the relationship. When this happens, amazing transformations can occur. When this kind of reconciliation occurs, it's a gift to be cherished.

2. **Shifting your expectations.** In this type of reconciliation, one person changes his or her expectations of the other person, and the relationship opens up, whether or not the other person makes significant changes.

3. **Agreeing to disagree.** In this instance, two people have dramatically different versions of past history--like whether or not abuse occurred--and rather than each trying to convince the other that they are right, they agree to disagree. They try to find common ground that isn't connected to the dispute as a way to forge a new relationship.

4. **Inner resolution.** This final kind of reconciliation is the inner path we travel when direct reconciliation with the other person is impossible. The other person may have passed away or may be too damaged or too hostile to make reconciliation possible. The other person may have slammed the door in your face and isn't about to open it anytime soon. Or you attempt reconciliation, and your efforts fail. In these instances, our task is to accept it and move one.

All four of these types of reconciliation highlight the foundation of grace—*Acceptance*. We accept the way things are, and the way they are not. To this end, we can be in right relationship with the truth, and make powerful choices based on truth. Even if the truth hurts.

Britannica defines reconciliation as *the process of finding a way to make two different ideas, facts, etc., exist or be true at the same time.* Grace is a pathway that makes this possible. To hold grace for another person means that you accept them as they are—without it meaning anything about *you*. It means that if they do something wrong in your opinion, it doesn't define their whole humanity, nor does it define yours. I think about my best friend who, as a Black man, voted for the other guy in 2016. I was both dumbfounded and heart broken. For me, this was an absolute breach of every value I hold sacred. Our relationship *had* to be over. I stepped away and took some time to process his decision. After a while, I had to consider the 20+ years of friendship and the value he brought to my world. I had to figure out a way for that decision not to define his entire existence, his humanity, and honestly his sanity. I had to grapple with the question, "how can his voting decision *co-exist* with my love for him?" I chose grace.

We made an agreement to never, ever, ever speak about politics. We knew that was a danger zone for us. I'll be honest and say that to this day, I still get sick thinking about his decision, but I also let him deal with that, and I stick to the business of being his friend. Admittedly, we are not *as* close as we were, but I know he has my back and I certainly have his...always.

Reconciliation is like a truing up of sorts and can look many ways. It can be an Executive Director acknowledging historical harm that have been made in the organization, it can look like two coworkers finding a way to gracefully agree to disagree, or it can look like a manager *finally* terminating that problematic employee in the name of peace, productivity, and healing for the rest of the team, or it can look like leaving an organization for your own health and wellbeing.

CHAPTER 3 – GRACE IN THE PUBLIC SQUARE

In 2022, a Black woman planned an outing for her two young nieces to a Sesame Street-based theme park, Sesame Place. When a person dressed as the character Rosita came upon a crowd of adults and children, the character can be seen greeting children, shaking their hands, and patting their heads. But as "Rosita" approached the Black girls, the human in the costume waved his or her hands in a motion commonly associated with the word "no". (Jodi, 2022) Many felt that gesture signaled that the Rosita character did not want to interact with the Black children, despite having done so with children of other ethnicities who were present at the time. The public outcry prompted Sesame Place to release three "apologies." Notice the evolution of tone in each:

Apology #1
Video goes viral
"The knee-jerk denial"

> *"The performer portraying the Rosita character has confirmed that the 'no' hand gesture seen several times in the video was not directed to any specific person, rather it was a response to multiple requests from someone in the crowd who asked Rosita to hold their child for a photo which is not permitted."* (Sesame Place, 2022)

The release of an additional photo (NBC Philadelphia News, 2022) from a different angle proves this statement as false, showing no one else in the line of sight for the mascot, and the mascot hugging a white child right after passing the little girls.

Apology #2
Video is more widely spread and public outrage increases
"The admission and symbolic gesture of accountability"

> *"We sincerely apologize to the family for their experience in our park on Saturday; We know that it's not ok. We are taking actions to do better. We are committed to making this right. We will conduct training for our employees, so they better understand, recognize, and deliver an inclusive, equitable and entertaining experience to our guests."* (Sesame Place, 2022)

This statement was largely rejected by the public as people continued to view and share the video. It wasn't until multiple other videos surfaced that appeared to show similar incident of Black children being shunned by employees playing characters at the park, and the family's decision to engage a civil rights attorney, that Sesame Place gave a final apology:

Apology #3
Family retains a lawyer
"The back-against-the-wall ownership"

> *"We have been in contact with the family since Sunday morning and we remain in contact through their lawyer, Mr. LaMarr. We have offered to meet the family and their attorney in person, as early as today, to personally deliver an apology and an acknowledgement that we are holding ourselves accountable for what*

happened. We want to listen to them to understand how the experience impacted their family and to understand what we can do better for them and all guests who visit our parks. We are committed to learning all we can from this situation to make meaningful change. We want every child who comes to our park to feel included, seen and inspired.

We are taking action and are reviewing our practices to identify necessary changes, both in the immediate and long-term. We are instituting mandatory training for all of our employees so that we can better recognize, understand, and deliver an inclusive, equitable and entertaining experience for all our guests. We have already engaged with nationally recognized experts in this area.

We take this extremely seriously; we are heartbroken by what these young girls and this family experienced in our park. It is antithetical to our values, principles and purpose. We are committed to working tirelessly and intentionally to make this situation better. We will do the necessary work for the long haul -- not just in the public eye, but also behind the scenes and within ourselves." (CBS News Philadelphia, 2022)

This is the dance organizations engage in when faced with their apparent racism. It is the kind of overt gaslighting where the organization denies the public the right to trust what they saw and heard together with the accounts of those who were present during the incident. They whitewash the facts and protect the wrongdoer. In doing so, however, they affirm the culture that breeds episodes like the one the world saw at a theme park for children!

The last statement released by Sesame Place left too many questions unanswered:

1. Was the employee reprimanded or fired?
2. What was the "necessary work" the company was committing to do?
3. Was the first apology a lie? Either the leadership lied, which they didn't admit, or the employee lied, who, as of this writing, is still working for Sesame Place. Which is it?
4. Would it make a difference if the performer was Black? Or white? Would it matter? Why? Since we don't know how the person wearing the costume racially identifies, it's interesting to think about how that information would figure into our reaction to the crisis.

This situation provides a powerful case study on organizational racism and could have been a remarkable opportunity for Sesame Place to address what seem to be deeply rooted, systemic issues of racism within the organization. Instead, they promised bias training but failed to say in either statement that the park already had courses in bias training which one would assume the "Rosita" performer took. Additional bias training is not a solution.

This story caught the eye of Forbes magazine contributor, Janice Gassam Asare, (Asare, 2022) who recommended the following to the leaders at Sesame Place and its parent company, Sea World, in part:

> Prior to hiring anyone at Sesame Place, or any other workplace, there should be anti-racist hiring practices baked into the hiring process… It's important to also understand that being from

a racially marginalized background doesn't prevent someone from buying into oppressive systems like colorism and anti-blackness. Who is evaluating job candidates? Is there a diverse panel of people assessing candidates? Having more people helping with the decision-making process can mitigate potential bias, but it's imperative that those involved in the process are part of diverse communities. Are employees being evaluated based on diversity, equity and inclusion metrics? Think about including questions in employment interviews to assess candidate awareness when it comes to diversity, equity, and inclusion. Consider introducing policies that make it clear that racist behavior will not be tolerated and that discrimination will carry swift and immediate consequences.

The article went on to suggest other measures the theme park might consider taking like customer evaluations and appraisals. By giving the customer a voice and asking how their visit to the theme park was, the organization could have identified that there were issues with apparent bias with other employees dressed as characters. Of course, other video and testimony have now surfaced to allege there are multiple similar incidents.

That said, simply asking the customers about their experiences is hardly sufficient if the data that is received is explained away, ignored, kept secret, or never evaluated in a meaningful way. And how would the customer know that if it was or wasn't considered? They would likely never know the impact of their rating.

The Sesame Place incident set up an opportunity for organizational catharsis, but the company missed it entirely, leaving those who have been victimized to wonder if there is any chance for the kind of equity we hope for.

White Supremacy at Sesame Place

White Supremacy is commonly demonstrated in organizations in the following ways:

1. **Lack of Ownership and Recognition** - The organization demonstrated an inability to evaluate its own culture and recognize inappropriate behavior taking place right under the leadership's nose.
2. **Lack of Empathy** - The organization demonstrated an inability to sympathize, comprehend, or relate to how their racist acts, whether big or small, impact others.

3. **Lack of Accountability and Action (until monetary consequences are threatened)** - The organization's inaction by leaders in the face of accusations or evidence of racism revealed a propensity to sweep things under the carpet or try to talk the accuser down from their complaint until litigious and/or monetary threats are made. In many cases, gaslighting is a common tactic where obvious acts of racism are downplayed as nothing of concern.

Sesame Place unfortunately did all three. One of the primary issues people of color have experienced is that white people, especially those in power, don't have the capacity to empathize. Even when they clearly cause harm or pain, there seems to be no connection to what it must feel like for those on the receiving end.

Enter grace.

Grace equity would have morally compelled Sesame Place to acknowledge humanity and harm <u>from the beginning</u>. They would have confessed that their practices and policies around racism have been, at the very least, neglected and, at the worst, encouraging of such behavior. What else would explain why an employee would have such comfort behaving so egregiously toward children knowing that parents and others were filming with their smartphones? The employee may have been emboldened by the fact that previous incidents went unacknowledged.

Also, there would have been a public opportunity for people to witness the full *circle of truth and reconciliation* had there been any or all of the following:

- A sincere acknowledgment by Sesame Place of the employee's behavior
- An authentic apology
- An opportunity extended to the family to allow Sesame Place to make it right
- A public reconciliation where the parents could acknowledge their own anger and pain, yet still recognize that Sesame Place satisfactorily restored them to wholeness.
- A clear articulation of what steps would be taken to ensure that this doesn't happen again.

Sesame Place, like so many other organizations, educational institutions, governments, and others, missed their moment. And now that the damage is done, nothing they do will seem to be enough.

What we as the public rarely get to experience is restoration when outcry is met with lies and obfuscations. Radio silence by companies is the most common ploy in the end - precisely what happened with Sesame Place after its many apologies.

Organizations just wait for something else to distract the world and return to business as usual. We are left with a world of injustice and without a model of how to heal one another person to person, company to person, and company to company. Activating grace is the solution. It makes change, reconciliation, and justice available.

CHAPTER 4 – GRACE, WOKENESS, AND CANCEL CULTURE

Wokeness

First, I'll start with a little history about the evolution of the term "woke." The following timeline is cited in the Washington Post (Bayne, 2022).

> The earliest known examples of wokeness as a concept date back to the 1920's and centered around the idea of Black consciousness and power. It encouraged Black people to "wake up" to their collective power and stand up for their own freedom and communities.
>
> It started in 1923 when philosopher and social activist, Marcus Garvey, encouraged Black people to become more socially and politically conscious. He offered a speech where he exclaimed, "Wake up, Ethiopia! Wake up, Africa!"
>
> In 1938, the term "stay woke" was part of a song by Blues singer Huddie Ledbetter who sang about nine Black teens in Arkansas accused of raping two white women.
>
> Decades later, in 1970, the Black-nationalist rappers, the Last Poets, recorded the song "Wake Up N***er."

A 1972 play entitled "Garvey Lives!" by playwright Barry Beckham included the line: "I been sleeping all my life. And now that Mr. Garvey done woke me up, I'm gon' stay woke."
1988 brought the iconic *School Daze* movie by Spike Lee. Campus activist Dap, played by Laurence Fishburne, screamed, "Wake up!!!" in rebuke of Black people, encouraging them to unify rather than be divided.

In 2014, the term became re-popularized by Black Lives Matter after the shooting of Michael Brown in Ferguson, Missouri.

In 2016, BET aired the Black Lives Matter documentary about the power of Black people telling their own stories. The name of the film was *Stay Woke*.

Just a one year later in 2017, "woke" entered the Oxford English Dictionary.

In response to many of the events that occurred in 2019 and 2020, most notably the murder of George Floyd, wokeness became mainstream and is now currently used primarily in reference to white people who want to signal that they are aware of the racial prejudice that exists in America and are on the good side of the fight.

With the appropriation of wokeness by white people, we have entered "The Woke Movement" which is now showing up in politics, social movements, and organizational structures. But in an attempt to steer out of a skid, many organizations appeared to have overcorrected and crashed.

For starters, levels of wokeness became a basis for bragging rights. Competing for the most "woke" award grew into a kind of social sport. Time and time again, I have seen white people pilloried by other white people who have become the watchdogs for all things social justice. They have been castigated for saying something that is inappropriate, offensive, or not consistent with current standards of speech.

I discovered this when I was at a conference with about 300 people in attendance. There were two white women in particular who kept correcting others and calling them out for the terminology they were using – or as they said, "calling them in."

For example, one of the panelists used the term, "differently-abled" and one of the women corrected them by saying that people in the disabled community didn't like that term, and actually preferred if people used the term "disabled." These interruptions and confrontational outbursts by the women continued over the course of the two days of the conference.

As I surveyed further. I also noticed that they were only correcting other white people. I had to wonder why they were choosing their targets so selectively.

Finally, I overheard one woman say to the other, "I really thought that with a Black woman hosting this training, the panelists would have been more woke."

This seems to be a trend where many white people expect to gain some status, superiority, and "street cred" by using the right jargon when referring to people from marginalized groups. They often suppose that it identifies them as advocates for the work of race equity and gives them license to beat up on other white people by over-policing their language, judging their level of "wokeness," and, consequently, creating an environment that is miserable for other white people to feel open and willing to share themselves. It is miserable for folks of color to bear witness to as well.

I would want the "woke" white folks, especially in organizations, to know a few things:

1. Your wokeness and bullying of other white folks can be harmful to people of color. First, when you are "calling in" a white person, it is often assumed that you are representing the interests and voices of people of color. The Black community is not a monolith. Just like white people, we all have different lived experiences and perspectives, so not only are you being arrogant to assume you know enough to check other white folks, but you are also taking a reductionist approach that enforces stereotypes and assumptions. I would ask that you think about your motive before interjecting. If it is about opening dialogue as an opportunity to better understand each other from YOUR OWN lived experience then great. But, often, it's nothing more than virtue signaling and taking up space.

2. Please understand the level of arrogance you boast if you act on behalf of people of color who haven't asked you to. Please consider that it's really another form of white supremacy and many folks of color feel it. We can tell when you are speaking with us, for us, or against us.

3. It is infantilizing to step in and fight the battles of other adults. It assumes people of color cannot or should not fight their own battles. Rather than showing support and solidarity, this behavior belittles those who you intended to defend, and you appear insensitive in your speech or behavior.

4. When speaking for "the community," it can be assumed that you aren't speaking for yourself. This is problematic in that it removes you from the narrative. In this way, you don't have to own your thoughts, feelings, and beliefs. You can always say, "I'm doing this for the community."

Instead, consider a different approach. If you are in a meeting and you see or hear something problematic, rather than saying people of color are often not included in these decisions and may feel this way or that way, try speaking for yourself with a phrase like, "I can't speak for anyone in this meeting, but when I hear your perspective, it makes *me* concerned that we haven't considered all voices." This shows that you are personally invested in the outcome, not just telling the room what you think "the community" might say.

Of course, you may be collaboratively engaged in community spaces where you are asked to advocate because you are positioned with power and/or access. This is a completely different scenario where you might represent the thoughts and feelings of a group.

What the two women in the conference did was to cause the other attendees in the room to be guarded, uneasy, and afraid to speak. This is the opposite of what is most needed right now. While they might have gained hyper-awareness about terminology and past racist harms, they lacked the essential element of grace.

They might have better served the conversation by abandoning the measure of how much more woke they were than the next white person. People come to understand and acknowledge their hidden racism in many ways and different timeframes. Their understanding unfolds over time.

Instead, what these ladies might have done was commit to demonstrating their wokeness with their actions by making a difference in their corner of the world. I so wanted to ask them how many Black friends they had, how many Black causes they had supported, and how many times they had welcomed Black folks into their inner circles, their parties, their churches, and their community organizations. After all, what's the sense of being woke in one's conversation if it doesn't result in making the world a better place for the very people you claim to be waking up to?

I want people to understand that, in the grand scheme of race equity work, no one has it all figured out, mostly because the conversation of race is driven by the news media, articles, interviews, the word on the street, kitchen table, water cooler, hearsay, and books that tell people what others think, feel, and experience. Very few learnings come from real cross-racial dialogue. Such conversations must be held in spaces where we can humanize each other. Without the humanization that grace brings, I will always be just a Black woman instead of a human that happens to be Black. Even those of us who practice in this space are learning something new every day. There is no stable for high horses in this fight as there is so much for us all to learn.

So, what is the result of all the wokeness sweeping across America? More stereotyping, more bullying, more arrogance, and a whole bunch of folks being shamed and feeling "forced" to attend diversity and inclusion trainings. Many white folks feel like they are being forced to admit what monsters they are. Has this made life for people of color significantly better? I'd argue that it has not. I believe we completely missed the point and blew the opportunity to realign to a bigger, more blessed vision for our organizations and institutions. We forgot to inject the element of grace that allows us to be honest about where we are, truthful about our ignorance on how to move forward, and humble enough to ask, "What should I do next?"

People, governments, countries, and organizations need a new way to approach the conversation of race in a way that fosters and promotes reconciliation. Beating up others to get them to see the light has not gotten the job done. A new approach is required. Grace is that new approach.

Cancel Culture

Cancel culture refers to the growing method of withdrawing support or demonstrating disagreement with a person, place, or thing. When a public figure, or company has done or said something objectionable or offensive, they are *canceled*. The result of canceling can be anything from the termination of a job such as a college professor who is fired, perhaps a demand to remove a comedian from a network or stop his or her tour, or demand that a company like Sesame Place close their doors. Canceling typically looks like group shaming and/or silencing the voice of a person or entity.

How is this different from the woke culture? While woke culture is about raising voices; cancel culture is about silencing voices.

There are many different views of cancel culture as a form of activism. Here are some pros and cons:

PROs

- Cancel culture is considered a powerful tool of power-balancing for those with no power. It is a way for an individual to say, "I may not have the same systemic, structural, political, economic, or social power as you, but if I band together with these 10 million other folks, we can collectively hold you accountable for your wrongdoing." This is especially true when the justice system has failed. A perfect example of this would be disgraced R&B singer, R. Kelly, who was a known pedophile and skirted justice for decades. He now sits in jail serving a 30-year sentence because of the #metoo and #muteRKelly movements.

- In addition to holding people accountable, cancel culture is also a tool for giving voice to those who don't have the power to speak their truths as individuals. The #metoo movement allowed women who had been living with secrets of sexual abuse and harassment the collective platform to stand up along with millions of other women and share their stories.

- Canceling creates a mechanism for people to dissent against injustice and inequality safely and privately. Many people take to the streets, but for those who are unable to express their anger or frustration in this way, social media and online expression can be a powerful tool for accessible activism.

CONs

- Canceling has no inherent mechanism for dialogue. When we rush to cancel someone, we leave no room to hear their stories, and we disregard the many complexities of the human experience. Without this dialogue or ability to humanize each other, we cannot move forward together as a society. No one learns, and all that is left is a kind of societal pouting: "I don't like what you said or did;" "I don't want to know why you think and feel the way you do;" "I just want you to disappear." And isn't this exactly what white supremacy is all about?

Instead of white supremacy, we are now engaging in social supremacy. When we have a group of people who believe their values and beliefs are paramount to the extent that they feel justified in cutting off another person's livelihood, this can become a very slippery slope toward the very society we don't want. A society in which one group of people can say "my way, is THE way" without question or dialogue with one another sounds like white supremacy to me.

- It assumes that people can't learn from their mistakes. Who gets to judge someone as unredeemable? When we cancel, we are making the ultimate decision about one's capacity for growth and redemption. We don't encourage people to acknowledge their wrong. Instead, we force them into defensive mode. I'm sensing a theme here. Yup, white Supremacy.

  In the rare cases when people admit their wrong and apologize, society deems the apology insincere or insufficient, and the person often gets canceled anyway.

  The very idea of this suggests that a person, or group of people, can judge whether or not others can learn, change, or grow. It assumes that this person's mistake is unforgivable while their detractors continue to make mistakes day after day. You might remember the saying, "He who is without sin, cast the first stone!" You already know what I'm going to say. Oh heck, I'll say it anyway. This is some straight up white Supremacy, y'all!

- It leaves no room for nuance. Without dialogue or knowing other people's story, how can anyone determine the heart of another? We ALL have had thoughts, feelings, and engaged in behavior we are not proud of. So, who gets to determine which ones rise to the level of cancellation? I wonder how many of us would be canceled if we had all our business out in the streets like famous people. Just wondering folks... just wondering.

- There isn't any rubric or metrics on what is cancellable. It appears to be a very discretionary, movable target. Recently we watched Will Smith slap Chris Rock at the Oscars. I was waiting for the #cancelWill hashtag. It never came. Perhaps the #canceltoxicmasculinity hashtag? Nope.

Still nothing. What I and many others knew was that Will Smith is going to be just fine. His charisma and blazing star power will save him. He will bounce back and most will ultimately embrace him again.

Many people, like me, read his book, and this shaped our understanding and perception of the infamous slap. I likely would have felt differently had I not known his life story. And therein lies a huge difference. One's personal story helps us make sense of their actions. And when we can make sense of a person's actions, we are more able to extend grace to them. Even those of us who condemned Will's actions that day were not willing to cancel him because we knew his story.

I'm not sure if cancel or woke culture is here to stay. I imagine just like disco, valley girls, and parachute pants, it's not. But for now, I would just hope that if there is something we don't like about someone's personal choices or beliefs, except violence or abuse, we try to raise concerns in a way that opens dialogue and moves us all forward, as opposed to shutting people down and blocking their ability to earn a living, especially, if we don't know the story behind those beliefs and values.

CHAPTER 5 – THE ROLE OF GRACE AND RACE IN THE NONPROFIT SPACE

All my clients, except for one, are nonprofits. I really enjoy working with nonprofits because they are strongly beholden to their mission. Unlike for-profit entities that are driven by their stockholders and bottom lines, I find that nonprofits are typically driven by their mission, are nimbler, and can make more space for change in their organizations.

There are many dynamics of nonprofits that aid in their ability to engage in race equity work with more grace. However, there are some challenges that most organizations will inevitably confront when doing this work. The following seven challenges are a compilation of shared stories from fellow race equity consultants and the personal experiences I wrote about in my book, *Trust the Process*.

1. Fear of Change

One constant in life (and organizations) is change. Some things, like budgets, are out of our control and can force changes that organizations need to react to. But there are other changes that organizations *choose* to make – like institutionalizing equity into their organizational fabric. Either way, people generally resist change, and this resistance can weigh heavy on the head of the leaders. Also, because this change is related to a subject as anxiety-producing as race/race equity, we have to be especially deliberate in how we think things through. It takes a lot of adjusting and reframing to get into a rhythm and gain some traction. This requires a great deal of grace and vulnerability on the leadership's part to move with the "will of the people," which isn't always easy.

Speaking of grace and vulnerability, as a leader, you'll need a great deal of it because this work (and any kind of organizational change) is largely based on learning, being transparent, making mistakes, and being willing to adjust. What I find is that most leaders don't understand what it takes to do this work. They underestimate the scope of the change that needs to occur and, therefore, fail. Worse, they assume that they have some inherent protections due to the nature of the business: charity. They forget that, though the charity space may draw more philanthropic mindsets, much of that does not extend to race.

The result is that what leaders think is happening in their organization and what they think the work of equity is going to entail is a far cry from what actually happens and what they learn in the process.

What leaders think	What we know	What to do
I can just tell my staff that "We are now going to prioritize race equity in our work" and people will change.	Change often requires a shift in culture which can't be changed with simple communication.	Deliver many, many messages, all with a consistent theme and vision. Work as a leadership body to develop consistent talking points about this shared vision.
"We've been doing this for a year. We should be farther ahead by now." Or "It seems like things	Slow, steady, and CONSISTENT wins this race.	Set and manage expectations that this is long-term, holistic work. Be transparent about how much this

are actually getting worse! What gives?"		work can suck sometimes and that's just part of it. Don't pretend that "everything is just fine" when it isn't. Name the discomfort and anxiety.
I can do this work with the same people and the same structures.	The structures and/or people will need to adjust to do this work. Trying to implement new ideas with the same people, attitudes, behaviors, and structures will not work.	Expect some people who were are aligned with this work to leave. This happens. Implement structural changes that we'll address in a later chapter.

Finally, and probably one of the most important factors in managing fears and resistance to change is making sure to have effective *change managers* in place. These folks are put in place to anticipate and handle fear and resistance of the staff during change. I believe that the key is to *expect fear* and conflict, and then make sure to have the right players in place to handle it when it happens. Ideally, change management could look like this:

Senior Leadership/Leadership Team - The voice of change. Keeps a consistent message of the vision. Acknowledges resistance and makes a compelling case for the need to stay on course during times of change.

Middle Management - The voice of support. These are the managers who lead teams of staff and serve as a conduit for the

Director's voice. They will manage resistance by openly, actively, and consistently rearticulating *and modeling* the Director's message and vision to their teams.

Change Manager - The voice of action. This person (typically the Equity Director) or group (DEI Committee) is on the frontlines of the work. They keep the ball moving down the field and does the legwork of implementing and managing the practical pathways to fulfill the Director's vision of race equity.

If I could highlight anything from this section, it is the need for leadership to normalize fear *and* resistance to change. Don't run away from it, which will feel the most instinctive.

Preparing people upfront for resistance shows that as an organization you are capable and supportive of people having their own experiences throughout the process. **Managing** the change with consistent communication and opportunities for staff to give input promotes clarity and buy-in. Consistently and formally **revisiting and reflecting** on race equity work throughout the lifecycle provides a framework to continuously deal with resistance or fears that may be active or lying dormant.

2. Holding Senior Staff Accountable to the Work

This section could have gone under the above category of Fear of Change. However, because of its prevalence and impact on the work of race equity, it deserves its own section. I work with many different nonprofits, but I am going to use my experience with nonprofit legal aid organizations to drive this section home. As someone who has worked with many Legal Aid firms, I see this all the time. There are attorneys who have been in these organizations for decades and have built their entire identity around their success as an advocate. They are brilliant and loved by their communities who come to know the attorney as their champion. These attorneys become very protective of "their way" of doing things. Because of their strong reputations and being so good at what they do, leaders struggle to hold them accountable to the work and changes of an organizational race equity movement. The organization then becomes divided. On one side, you have senior attorneys unwilling to make the necessary adjustments that are necessary to create equitable conditions. On the other side you have those who are actively engaged in the work and annoyed that the senior attorneys are "untouchable" and uninvolved in race equity work within the organization. I've seen situations where these beloved attorneys are not required to attend meetings, participate in important initiatives like race equity, or account for their time in ways that junior attorneys must. This is inequitable. To boot, most of these attorneys – and similarly many leadership team members in other nonprofits – are often white, so it feels even more racialized.

3. Managing the Optics

There are two kinds of *optics* people are familiar with in this work. The "optics" to *external stakeholders* leads organizations to want to "look like" they are doing the work, but they aren't making the adjustments it takes to shift an organizational culture. This is also known as the "check the box" method. The second form of optics that most leaders tend to ignore are the *internal optics*, which are related to how staff *interprets* the decisions and actions of leadership.

For the most part, people are "meaning-making" machines that are designed to protect themselves. When an event occurs, we observe it, assign meaning to it, (figure out what it *means* about us, or how it *affects* us) and then begin to behave in accordance with that meaning – not necessarily the facts. Also, it has been my experience that many people don't investigate their assumptions; instead, they react to them as a truth. This then leads to gossip.

To mitigate gossip, we must stay ahead of it by spending a lot of time upfront figuring out what is needed to report out. Over time, when we include the following information, we can, to some degree, mitigate the effects of misinterpretations and confusion that activated gossip:

1. **Why the change was made**
Lack of awareness of *why* things happen is probably the number one cause of organizational mistrust and tension. There are things you just can't say, like why the Black employee was suddenly terminated. It may cause suspicion, but it will surely cause more damage if information related to it is shared. But even in this case, it is still important to say that.

2. **How this will affect the person's/team's job role and security**
People don't have to make assumptions about how decisions affect them if you disclose the impact up front. Also, it sends a message that you are in tune to the concerns of the people who will most likely be affected by a potential change.

3. **Acknowledgment of staff concerns or past failures**
It's not enough to say, *"We are going to do equity work and here is my new vision,"* but it is equally important to say, *"I recognize that we have tried this before. We did this thing and that thing and we missed the mark. Here is what we are doing differently now..."* Like most things, when you try to step over past failures and just create a new policy, staff have no way to discern how this time will be different and may automatically distrust it.

A final note on managing optics: how people interpret anything is ultimately an individual phenomenon. Of course, we can turn to research to help us gain a broader understanding of some of the root causes of how and why different groups perceive things the way they do, but the best and most effective (not always the most efficient) way I find to manage optics is through personal conversations with staff. My former Director would schedule individual 15 or 30-minute conversations with every staff member twice per year – specifically to talk about our race equity work, giving them an opportunity to share their concerns or give feedback. She would also report back to the leadership team after her staff calls were completed and share any themes or concerns we needed to be mindful of. This may not work for your organization, but we found that it was worth the 12 hours to ensure that people had space to talk to her.

4. Staff Leaving

Whenever an organization is taking on a new initiative that causes a shift in the way things are done, or in organizational priorities, expect some people to leave. There is often a subset of staff in most organizations who benefit from "the way things used to be" and don't want to lose those benefits, so they may likely try to sabotage efforts and/or end up leaving the organization.

However, there are others who may not necessarily be aligned to the new organizational vision but *want or need to stay*. These folks fall into two categories:

- **They go along to get along.** Perhaps they love their work/the organization and don't want to leave. In some cases, it's not financially feasible to leave. Perhaps they see the value, but simply don't want to do the work of race equity as it gets in the way of "their real work." These people are usually more passive in their resistance or,
- **They actively resist.** Active resistance can range from criticizing the work/leadership, to disrupting the efforts of the work, spreading rumors or making false claims — especially race-related claims. I've seen organizations go

through tremendous turmoil under these circumstances, and I can't stress enough that managing staff who are engaged in this behavior should be a top priority as it has a serious impact on organizational safety, sanctity, and stability. As an aside, if this actively resistant staff is a person of color, I think it's important that leaders think critically about whether or not it's more important to keep misaligned staff in order to avoid the negative optics of letting go of a person of color, versus doing what is best for the organization.

5. Setbacks/Comebacks

Let me first say that there will likely be a moment when you question why you ever started this work and you'll want to quit. If you don't experience this moment, you're probably not doing the work. At the very least, there will be setbacks. You'll feel like you are making headway, people are communicating more, the affinity groups seem to be gelling and then, something will happen that will cause people to question everything.

In my former organization there was a challenging situation that occurred with a staff member of color. I can tell you, having been a part of the leadership team, that this situation had nothing to do with this staff member's race, but rather their performance. It was a clear call that I (and the rest of leadership) was fully aware of and agreed it needed to terminate them. It was an unfortunate decision that needed to be made and even though we were aware of the potential racialized optics of the decision, we all agreed it was the best decision to make.

Had I not been a part of the leadership team, I would have been highly suspicious of this being a race issue. This situation taught me that there are sometimes when you have to weigh the risks between a *negative optics* about a decision, or real harm being brought to your organization.

This is where honesty, transparency, and grace come in. I would say, acknowledge the breakdowns. If you commit to something and don't do it, acknowledge that you didn't do it. If you try something and it doesn't work, acknowledge that you missed the mark and let people know the new plan. People are highly aware when things go awry, so not acknowledging breakdowns makes them think that leadership is either not aware of what is going on in the organization or don't care. Either way, trust in leadership will erode.

When setbacks happen, people will likely say, "See, we haven't really made much progress. Here we are again." All that I know to do is to own it, clean it up, and repeat your message of hope and commitment toward this work.

5. Unchecked Biases Against Staff of Color

I am compelled to add that because many leaders hold a racialized analysis of behavior, often people of color behave/react in a way that is considered aggressive or resistant, whereas their white counterparts are labeled as assertive or confident. Staff of color are more likely to be addressed with *punitive* measures as opposed to white staff who are more likely given *restorative* opportunities. So, it is absolutely critical for leaders to be discerning and able to check their racial bias.

Here is where I'll make a quick plug for having a multi-racial leadership team so that there can be an objective/subjective analysis of the staff's behavior. While my former (white) director was actively committed to developing her racial analysis, she admittedly relied on the feedback and input from her team to help her think through the most effective decision for staff. For example, as a woman of color, there may have been some insight I could contribute through the lens of a Black woman that would help her see things from a different angle. The key here is for leaders to be able to have a wider lens to evaluate staff, their staff's behavior, and the best approach to respond to it. This is best done with a diverse leadership team who can bring broad perspectives, and a leader who *truly* considers their input.

With that said, not everyone is going to fit in with the mission and vision of your organization. I work with consultants around the nation who are coaching leaders on how to effectively manage staff members who are essentially bringing harm to their organizations. In some cases, these staff members are in leadership roles which makes it worse because they tend to hire people who share *their* vision, rather than the Director's/organization's vision. This only perpetuates harmful cycles and is why I argue for *cutting ties sooner rather than later*. However, many leaders, understandably, want to exhaust every option before terminating someone. But keeping toxic staff members on board often ends up costing more time and money on the back end dealing with consulting costs or even legal fees.

6. Hiring

One of the primary places where white supremacy occurs in nonprofit organizations is in the hiring process. When an organization doesn't acknowledge their own racism, it hires people who align with the racist system that is already in place ensuring that it is preserved for years to come.

To address this issue, many companies that truly want to hire fairly, diversify their staff, and ensure that people who harbor racist views are weeded out have taken the approach of widening the decision-making process in hiring to ensure that the vetting process is more thorough and less biased.

In these antiracist human resources paradigms, applications are reviewed by committee rather than an individual so that personal biases are tougher to hide. By moving from a person to a committee, people need to justify to the other members of the committee their reasoning for selecting or excluding applications.

Hiring decisions have historically been done in organizational darkness. No one knows how many people of color have applied and were rejected due to indicators on their resume that expose their ethnicity like:

1. Ethnic names that are more commonly used in the Black communities
2. The name of a predominantly Black college or an HBCU (historically black college or university)
3. An address in a neighborhood that is known to be predominantly Black
4. Organizational affiliations with charities that address Black causes
5. Fraternity and sorority affiliates with historically Black organizations

This has led to a trend in resume writing where Black applicants "whiten" their resumes so that they cannot be eliminated upon the recruiter's reading of their resume. Knowing that their ethnicity will be revealed on interview, they cling to a shred of hope that they will be able to impress the interviewer enough to move on in the process.

Resume whitening has been well-studied and shown to provide the applicant with double the chance of being called in for the interview. This is a sad reality in a world where organizations pride themselves on diversity and promote their inclusive culture.

These research findings should provide a
startling wakeup call for business executives: A

63

bias against minorities runs rampant through the resume screening process at companies throughout the United States. Discrimination still exists in the workplace. Organizations now have an opportunity to recognize this issue as a pinch point, so they can do something about it."

~ Katherine A. DeCelles, James M. Collins Visiting Associate Professor of Business Administration at Harvard Business School.

To prove the veracity of the resume whitening claims, a group of researchers fabricated 1600 resumes and forwarded them to actual organizations with positions available. The jobs were all entry-level to ensure experience would not play a major role and they chose 16 metropolitan U. S. cities so that the likelihood of regional impacts would be lessened.

Half of the resumes were crafted to include information that would reveal the ethnicity of the applicant. (For this study, both Black and Asian indicators were used.) The other half of the resumes were "whitened" so that they were scrubbed free of any revealing racial reference. Of course, fake phone numbers and email accounts were created so that they could track the applications and record which ones generated invitations to come in and interview for the job.

The scrubbed resumes had a much higher rate of activity, with recruiters calling upon them to visit and be interviewed. With qualifications being equal, the study showed that whitening resumes was an effective way to increase one's chances of getting a job. Only a mere 10 percent of resumes that included ethnically identifiable information were invited to interview. But the same resumes, when whitened, yielded a 25 percent callback. A similar result was found for indicators that were presumed to be Asiansounding. Only 11.5% of the ethnic resumes were invited. And 21% of the whitened versions were called.

Advances in artificial intelligence in the human resources space have made it possible for computers to process the initial group of candidates, selecting for education, experience, and motivators. However, depending on the programmer and the data sources they pull from, these systems have been reported to be more bias than humans in some cases. This said, a few of my clients have used them and have had great success.

This may have helped Sesame Place ensure they had applicants who loved children of all races. But what to do with those who fall through the cracks?

The second line of defense in terms of workforce perspective is to determine how an organization will free itself from those who refuse to embrace equity. This assumes that there have been attempts via coaching, training, or some other form of personal development regarding equity.

Leaders must think critically about whether it's more important to keep misaligned staff in order to avoid the negative optics of letting them go, or doing what is best for the organization. People whose behavior threatens the organization may actively resist dialogue and training, disrupt the efforts of the work, spread rumors or make false claims, or refuse to work with people of color by inventing reasons that don't stand up to scrutiny.

I've seen organizations go through tremendous turmoil under these circumstances and can't stress enough that working effectively with staff who are engaged in this behavior should be a top priority as it has a serious impact on the organizational safety, sanctity, and stability.

Discrimination in the workplace is a pervasive problem especially now that it has gone underground. It is far less acceptable to be outwardly racist than it was just a few decades ago. So, people who are unaccepting of other ethnicities have learned to tunnel down. They build alliances slowly and carefully. And those alliances are far stronger because they are built on the truth that one will not expose the other. Each becomes a safe space to vent to the other forging a stronger bond.

Organizations must become more adept at noticing the pinch points in their structure so that they can be addressed appropriately.

White supremacy in any organization that has such employees, volunteers, or other members will be detrimental to the cause since they will not look for what they are convinced doesn't exist. This is true even in organizations that claim to be pro-diversity. Using the terms such as "equal opportunity employer," "minorities encouraged to apply," or "pro-diversity" may give white people the false view that their organization is open and diverse. But those words are about as potent as "organic" on a bag of apples. It all depends on how the organization defines them and their level of commitment to embedding them into the fabric of the organization.

Worse, when Black applicants and other people of color see these welcoming terms, they get a false sense of security that the company is open to their application and that it will be an antiracist environment to work in should they get the job offer. Neither is guaranteed by the mention of these socially acceptable terms. Applicants let their guard down because of the labeling and branding of the company. Many stop probing and observing to see if there is true diversity or just the promise of it — a promise that is never fulfilled. Such companies could have the same amount of discrimination as others that don't make diversity claims. It could even be worse because of the arrogance that comes with the notion that an organization is diverse just because it says it is. It assumes that everyone knows what the words mean and will act accordingly. They fail to check for understanding, measure for performance, and monitor progress.

Often, the person doing the initial interview is not the same as the person doing the screening and neither of these are likely to be the person writing the job post. So, while the person seeking a new employee in his or her department might be anti-racist, the people funneling applicants his or her way may not share those inclusive views. This is the disconnect that often occurs in organizations that lead to systemic isolation and rejection of people of color.

Cartoon artist, Manuel Pereyra, depicted the difference between success in the world as white person and success in the world as a Black person by drawing side-by-side, identical lanes on a racetrack. (NotInMyColour, 2022) The white person's lane is shown to be clear from the starting line to the finish line. But it is a very different picture for the Black person's lane. The racer is shown with an anvil chained to his ankle, alligators snapping at anything in the lane, and a huge river running across the middle of it. The artist's message was clear: the runner might make it to the finish line, but he'll be exhausted and bruised when he gets there. Running a race with the odds stacked against you leaves you exhausted even if you get the job. Knowing that you had to deny your heritage, a fundamental element of your person, changes your perception of the world.

These are some of the social pressures white people need to be aware of as they participate in the discussions about how to eradicate discrimination and create anti-racist organizational environments where people have the liberty to be who they are, called by their own names and identities, and proud of their backgrounds.

Discrimination in hiring has been an ongoing American problem since the end of slavery. And pointing it out to an organization is a tough responsibility since most have a kind of corporate arrogance that insists such racism cannot exist in their organization. It has been so ingrained in the day-to-day operations, it is nearly imperceptible to those who benefit from it or who perpetrate it. But to those who are victimized by it, it is plain to see.

Centering Antiracism

Change comes slowly in a large organization and cracks in the foundation allow racism to seep in even in those places where it has been carefully rooted out. Like weeds, it wants to keep growing back and must be consistently eradicated. By performing regular checks with all employees, organizations can hold the line on its antiracism policies and ensure new people coming are embedded with the right mindset.

Setting goals is another critical cog in the wheel of grace equity. By deciding from the start what the organization should look like, feel like, and act like, organizations leave less room for error, management changes, cultural apathy, and individual opinions. These goals should be measurable, written, specific, and time-bound so that the end zone is always in view. Goals that are so abstract and esoteric that they cannot be measured help no one and never give the organization (the people) any sense of accomplishment.

Anti-racism strategies must rise to the top of every organization's priority list. Why? Setting aside the moral argument that it is the right thing to do, organizations must recognize that consumers have discovered their power. They are not as easy to spoon feed as they once were when they had minimal choice. The advent of the internet and free or low-cost shipping, people can vote with their feet and their wallets. They can choose to shop elsewhere. But, more than that, when a consumer writes off an organization, they don't go away quietly. They use their social media platforms to highlight the injustices they experienced. Such protests often go viral, costing the organization credibility, donations, sales, and/or reputation.

There is no place for white supremacist arrogance in a 21st century world. We are learning so much each day about each other, our communities, and the world at large. Humility with grace is the name of the game.

Working our way to unconscious competence

In the early 1970's, theorist Noel Burch developed a practical theory that describes how people learn. This theory is called "Four Stages of Learning". The stages are as follows (*cited from: Exceptional Leaders Lab* www.exceptionalleaderslab.com):

1. **Unconscious Incompetence**—The individual does not understand or know how to do something and does not necessarily recognize the deficit. They may deny the usefulness of the skill. The individual must recognize their own incompetence, and the value of the new skill, before moving on to the next stage. The length of time an individual spends in this stage depends on the strength of the stimulus to learn.
2. **Conscious Incompetence**—Though the individual does not understand or know how to do something, he or she does recognize the deficit, as well as the value of a new skill in addressing the deficit. The making of mistakes can be integral to the learning process at this stage.
3. **Conscious Competence**—This individual understands or knows how to do something. However, demonstrating the skill or knowledge requires concentration. It may be broken down into steps, and there is heavy conscious involvement

in executing the new skill.

4. **Unconscious Competence**—The individual has had so much practice with a skill that it has become "second nature" and can be performed easily. As a result, the skill can be performed while executing another task. The individual may be able to teach it to others, depending upon how and when it was learned.

We all seek to be unconsciously competent, that is, we want to get to a place where we don't have to think about what we know. For example, where leaders have a strong handle on the organization and understand the heartbeat that sustains it. Racism and inequity are an afterthought because the organization is diverse and equitable in pay and promotion. Its monitoring systems are consistent and yield positive feedback. Conversations occur regularly to address new concerns. And people feel like they are heard and valued.

But before we get there — to that blessed promised land — we are unconsciously incompetent because <u>we don't know what we don't know</u>. There is so much going on around us that we cannot and do not perceive. We require intense care to address the ills of the organization. The stage after unconscious incompetence is conscious incompetence. In this stage, <u>we know that we don't know</u>. This is a humbling place, but it is where learning begins. It is also where grace thrives. When you know what you don't know, you ask questions, listen intently, read, watch, discover, explore.

Organizations almost always need help to reach this plateau. Trying to resolve racism from within the organization risks putting people at risk and subsequently in defense mode. They have a personal or professional stake in the outcome, so they are less likely to be able to resist the urge to make it all look better than it is. Bringing in a trusted professional from the outside will help establish perspective, objectivity, accountability and, yes... grace.

The bottom line is that nonprofits deal with many of the same struggles as corporate leaders in the for-profit space, perhaps more, because people who work in this space aren't expecting to have to deal with them at all. But by making changes in hiring, policy, and mindset, these challenges serve as steppingstones to make the nonprofit a more dynamic place to work, further enhancing its work and mission.

CHAPTER 6 – QUIET RACISM

I was in my front yard doing some yard work when one of my neighbors walked past my house and smiled. I smiled back and offered a friendly wave. I noticed him turn around and come toward me.

"I want to thank you for something," he said.

I looked at him politely without responding, partly because I was giving him the space to speak, but mostly because I wanted to make it clear that I wasn't really interested in actively engaging.

He continued, "I just want to say that you really keep your yard and home so nice. I really feel like a total ass because I've had some really strong beliefs about living among Black neighbors, and you've completely made me take a long hard look in the mirror about how I judge and make assumptions based on these stereotypes. I'm sorry, and thank you."

In this moment I had to do what many Black women must do at least 10 times a day: make a decision about how to respond or whether I should respond to this at all. Because, let's be honest, that was some ignorant mess, offered in the name of a compliment. Textbook microaggression, more specifically, a microinsult. Rather than say hello, get to know me, and start a friendly neighborly relationship, he threw up all over me. Then, with his discomfort from his *own* ignorance relieved, he left me to live with the stench. I know... gross.

My decision tree goes something like this:

- Option #1: Do I cuss him out and tell him what a racist thing that was to say?
    - No, we are the only Black family in my community, and I don't want to have to deal with the blowback of being the angry Black neighbor. As of right now, I get along with all my neighbors and if I tell him what is really on my mind and call him the "r" word, things will just get weird and that would change the dynamics. My home is my sanctuary – not worth it.

- Option #2: Do I embarrass him with some shade like, "Oh, so you're telling me that you are racist, and haven't wanted to live around Black folks, but thanks to me, you realize you're wrong, and are proud of yourself for figuring it out? So proud that you feel the need to let me know, and even apologize for something that I wasn't even present to until now? Do you know how arrogant it is that you think your personal revelation about Black people is so profound that it should be shared with Black strangers? Am I supposed to be proud that you approve of me as a credit to my race?"
    - No can do. This kind of response may provoke him to say something back to me. And nothing he says will be good. If he back pedals, I'll be annoyed, and if he doubles down, refer back to option #1.

- Do I tell my husband?
    - Absolutely not! I do not tell my proud, Black, protective, 6'3" husband who would likely go knocking on the neighbor's door demanding an apology to his wife. These kinds of situations end up in death for Black men.

- Do I meet him with grace and say, "I really get that you are complimenting me, but here is how that lands when you say things like that"? What you are doing is called exceptionalism, which means assuming I'm different from the norm. I'm different from other Black people who *are* bad neighbors. You are calling me an exception to the rule that Black people are not pleasant to live around."
    - No, I don't want to educate. I do this all day long and I'm off the clock. I just want to work in my yard in peace.

I answered with the most gracious answer I could muster, "OK." I turned away and continued to work in my yard.

What this man did was try to make himself feel good by letting me know that he came to terms with something that I had no clue about. He effectively dumped his conscience on me to feel lighter and better about himself. If he acted in grace, he would have seen me minding my own damn business and just offered a compliment:

- Those roses look lovely there.
- I love what you're doing with your house. I might try that at my place.
- Hi, neighbor, need a hand?

Anything other than these should be taken up with his therapist, white affinity group, partner, friend, or pastor. Anybody but the person you are judging.

What he did was act in fake revelation as if suddenly his eyes had been opened. But I believe that if another Black family moved to our street, they would have to prove themselves to him just as I, unwittingly, did. I could be wrong, but they would likely be subject to his biased eye on how well they kept up with their landscaping just as I was. They would have to deal with their child being asked,

"Oh, which house is yours?" which is code for, "Do you belong here?"

My neighbor didn't have any revelation. What he had was a surprise!

These kinds of microaggressions happen ALL the time in the workplace towards folks of color. The decision tree where a person of color has to weigh the risks of speaking their truth, even if it's in response to someone who clearly feels entitled to speak *theirs,* is a constant burden we bear.

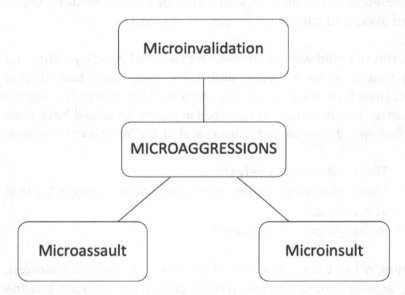

Because the term microaggressions was so broad, in 2007, Columbia University psychologist Derald Wing Sue proposed further classifications on the term *microaggressions*. They are as follows:

Microassaults: Conscious and intentional actions or slurs, such as using racial epithets, displaying swastikas or deliberately serving a white person before a person of color in a restaurant.

Microinsults: Verbal and nonverbal communications that subtly convey rudeness and insensitivity and demean a person's racial heritage or identity. An example is an employee who asks a colleague of color how she got her job, implying she may have landed it through an affirmative action or quota system. *Or a neighbor who praises his Black neighbor for keeping her home maintained.*

Microinvalidations: Communications that subtly exclude, negate, or nullify the thoughts, feelings or experiential reality of a person of color. For instance, white people often ask Asian-Americans where they were born, conveying the message that they are perpetual foreigners in their own land. Or crying or shaking when a Black woman raises their voice, but not reacting that way when a white woman raises their voice.

Microaggressions, from the lens of grace, might be explained this way: You say this, I hear that. For example:

MICROAGGRESSION	WHAT IS HEARD
Where are you from?	You aren't from here. You're an outsider.
You are a credit to your race.	Exceptionalizing; Others of your race aren't as smart.
I don't see color.	I don't respect your heritage.
I don't care if you are blue, purple, or green.	There are no blue people. You wish to deny something integral to my humanity.
You speak so well.	Most people like you don't speak well.
All lives matter.	I don't want to acknowledge history or that Black lives have been devalued.

I'm colorblind.	You don't want to acknowledge my race.
Smile! You should smile more often.	I don't know what to think when a Black person shows their resting face.

While there are times when microaggressions are deliberate, I would argue that more times than not, there is a genuine attempt to connect with the person they are offending. But if we don't find a way to have real dialogue about microaggressions, they will become increasingly more problematic and will soon turn into situations where people of color are left with no other option than to react and are set up to fail. Following are some of the problematic situations I've seen within the organizational context. I call them quiet racism because they are usually masked as "opportunity" or "deference."

Assign people of color in an organization to the committees on race within the organization. While these very people are not invited to address issues of corporate direction, marketing, hiring, etc., they are included when the topic of race is being addressed. Quiet racism.

Task people of color with coming up with the solutions to the systemic racism issues in the company. We have addressed this earlier in the book, but it bears repeating that racism is a white issue and demands a white response. Yes, thought leaders can dialogue with staff of color to help identify the problems and discuss solutions. But to put the weight of change on the shoulders of those who are harmed by these issues is *more harm*. White leaders, workers, and members of organizations must shoulder the burden themselves and quarterback the initiatives that bring about change while involving everyone in the discussion of what that change needs to look like.

Demand that all people of color participate in anti-racism training and use their unwillingness to participate as an excuse to terminate the discussion. Many people of color are exhausted from a lifetime of battling racism. They may or may not be willing to have yet another meeting, commit the time, expend the emotional energy it takes to repeat what they have been trumpeting for decades. Also, since most of these anti-racism trainings are centered on white behavior, there is no need for them to attend. Many of my clients don't require staff of color to attend these kinds of trainings. It is quiet racism to assume that all people of color in an organization should find the bandwidth to pull their white counterparts up the mountain that is racism.

Each member of the organization must be empowered to speak and encouraged to participate but forcing any person of color to share only exacerbates the very racism, in the form of quiet racism, one is trying to remove.

Unclear or unenforced polices in place for whistleblowers. Far too many people of color have spoken up about their concerns only to be fired, demoted, removed from the running for management, shunned, or ridiculed. And white people who dare to speak up are mocked and derided for being sympathetic and concerned. They are often warned that their own careers might be in jeopardy if they persist. Organizations must have clear policies about how racism is reported and to whom. I do not recommend a single point person for reporting. I've seen too many instances of an HR person who doesn't have a lens for equity and causes more harm when a person courageously comes forward. A small group of 3, for example, that is diverse in makeup is far better equipped to fairly respond to complaints.

White leaders giving "grace" to people of color in ways that potentially bring harm to organizations. A very common thing I see is white leaders who are unwilling or afraid to discipline people of color for poor performance or problematic behavior because they don't want to appear racist. Especially when the organization has made the commitment to antiracism and equity.

There was a client who called me in to guide them through the process of establishing equitable policies, practices, and culture. One of the most active and outspoken people in the movement was a woman of color. Unfortunately, the woman had been having serious performance concerns for some time, but now that she was one of the loudest voices on the subject of racism within the organization, leadership didn't know how to manage her performance without it appearing like she was being retaliated against for speaking truth to power. I shared with them that:

1. This is what happens when poor performance goes unchecked for too long and there are no clear structures in place for providing proper support when a staff member is struggling, and documentation of those supports being offered.

2. If she had been a white woman with the same concerns, there would have been little to no issue holding her accountable primarily based on her race.

Ultimately, leadership had to admit that they were afraid of this woman of color. They didn't discipline her because they were afraid and once she had a stronger platform and voice, they *really* didn't want to discipline her. In the meantime, other staff members picked up the slack for this woman and dealt with the blowback of her poor performance. They grew angry and resentful. Everyone knew this woman was problematic and yet, nothing was being done.

They were faced with either dealing with the growing frustration of other high-performing staff members and risk losing them or dealing honestly with this staff member. They decided to have a conversation with the problematic staff member, and they established a formal performance plan with very clear expectations and outcomes if those expectations weren't met. She claimed they were retaliating and were attempting to push her out. She gave notice four days later.

Again, this is not easy work. That is why grace must serve as the umbrella over it all. In this case grace would look like:

- Being honest with this woman *from the beginning* and giving her the tools and information to be successful. Recognizing that some people are deliberate detractors and distractors, but more times than not, people want to work and take care of themselves and/or their families. Before managing performance, check in to see if they need any accommodations or supportive measures. Take a humanity-first approach.

- Ensuring the psychological safety of the organization. If there is anyone who threatens the safety and sanctity of the organization, leadership must respond swiftly to send a message that 1) they see it, and 2) they are handling it; 3) certain behavior is not tolerated.

- The leadership body having a deep, honest reflection conversation about their implicit bias and fears related to people of color. Giving nonjudgmental space for them to name their concerns, biases, racism, or fears. This way, they can start holding each other accountable and provide support when they see each other behaving in ways that are racist, or inequitable or harmful.

Microaggressions continue to be a major barrier to grace equity. They occur so easily for some and are the result of a lifetime of conditioning such that they happen almost without the offender noticing. In every microaggression, there is an opportunity. When the instance happens in private settings, people of color have tough choices to make about addressing or choosing not to address them. In organizations, however, leaders can make it easier for people to talk about how they will be handled.

DARVO

I will dig into conflict in the following chapter, specifically addressing how organizations handle conflict. I'd be remiss if I didn't address the dynamics of interpersonal conflict when contextualized by race or racism. I will explain this through the framework of DARVO.

DARVO (Deny, Attack, Reverse Victim and Offender) is the work of Jennifer J. Freyed, a professor of psychology at the University of Oregon. This framework gives a name to the experience of too many people of color who are attempting to explain to a white person how their behavior and/or words are problematic or harmful. I will use the experience I shared about my neighbor as a model to demonstrate how DARVO plays out.

Suppose I chose option #3 – Grace. I might say, "I really get that you are complimenting me; but here is how that lands when you say things like you said. What you are doing is called exceptionalism, which means assuming I'm different from the norm. I'm different from other Black people who *are* bad neighbors. You are calling me an exception to the rule that Black people are not pleasant to live around."

Deny: "No that wasn't what I was saying. I would never say that. I was only trying to pay you a compliment."
- The goal is to destabilize you and chill the conversation
  – convince you that what you heard wasn't real, or what

82

you saw didn't happen, so they don't have to be accountable, and so that you second-guess yourself in future gaslighting situations.

Attack: "Not everything is about race. Why did you take something so innocent and turn it into something so hateful?"

- The goal is to disorient and discourage you - convince you that what you believe, feel, want and/or need is wrong, ignorant, unimportant, or even malicious, making it harder for you to stand your ground.

Reverse Victim and Offender: "I was only hoping to connect with you as my neighbor, but it seems you aren't interested in connection. Listen, I know that white men in this country are "the enemy," but perhaps, you can get to know me as a human, and not just a white man. My door is always open if you ever want to chat."

- The goal is to gaslight and shame you – convince you that you are the one bringing harm and set them up as the victim who deserves sympathy, compassion, and no consequences.

A public example of DARVO was displayed in Gayle King's interview with disgraced R&B artist, R Kelly. He denied ever abusing underage girls, and women. Next, he attacked his victims, calling them groupies and gold diggers looking to exploit his fame. Then he flipped the script in an Oscar-worthy performance as he screamed out sobbing about his innocence, "Stop it. Y'all quit playing! Quit playing! I didn't do this stuff! This is not me! I'm fighting for my f***ing life! Y'all killing me with this sh*t!"

Darlene Lancer, author and therapist, recommends that the best approach to DARVO is JADE.

- Don't **Justify**
- Don't **Argue**

- Don't **Defend**
- Don't **Explain**

I would like to add a 5th element – Don't **React** in response to the distracting behavior of crying, yelling or other forms of dominating. This was beautifully displayed by Gayle King in her interview with R Kelly. As he stood over her with his explosive and threatening tantrum, Gayle remained seated, poised, and calm. She simply repeated his name, "Robert, Robert, Robert." When I first saw the interview, I was glued to the TV, clapping my hands yelling, "Yes, Gayle! Do NOT fall for it, girl!"

DARVO centers around the tactic of gaslighting. But the JADE+R approach is the most self-gracious way to respond when you are being gaslit. Gaslighters are good at what they do and thrive on your engagement. If you don't engage, you remove their power.

Most racism is quiet. Quiet racism is subtle, difficult to see, and very difficult to prove. This is why it is so easy to be gaslit by racists, and those unwilling to see or admit to racist dynamics. But, in most cases, people of color see it with crystal clarity.

My appeal to leaders, especially white leaders, is to explore the ways in which DARVO operates within your organization and within you as the leader.

Ask yourself when and where you have seen it and how you might have handled the situation differently? Ask whether the white people in your organization feel at ease when behaving within the DARVO context knowing that they will be affirmed by you and others and shielded from having to self-reflect and evolve. Ask whether the people of color in your organization bear the constant burden of quiet racism while trying to be productive members of the corporate team.

CHAPTER 7 – DOING THE WORK

Racism must be dismantled swiftly. Yes, I did say earlier that this is work that takes time. However, the decision to act must be instant and the work must begin immediately thereafter. Because racism is so deep, moving swiftly is the only way to ensure that enough positive momentum is gained to make a difference in the lives of the current members of the organization. Otherwise, 30 years from now, the organization will be having the same conversations with no measurable change.

We have explored ways to combat racism in hiring, management, and training. And while it is important to note that initiatives are always exciting at first, the true work is in remaining vigilant in the weeks, months, and years after implementation. I can't tell you how many times I've entered organizations where the race equity team, typically 6-8 staff members, are meeting every week and have the loftiest of goals. I hate to have to be the wet blanket and request that they meet every other week and make their goals more feasible. This is because I walk in thinking about 5 to 10 years from now, when most of these folks won't be here. It is so important to set this process up for success.

Diverse Candidate Pipelines and Pools

While no organization should adopt a quota system, establishing goals to increase the presence of people of color in positions of leadership is a worthy aim. This should happen, though, as a natural result of implementing the protocols we have discussed. By diversifying the talent pool, it is easy to diversify the leadership positions.

Many companies turn to HBCUs, for example, searching for the best and brightest in the graduating class and wooing them into interviewing with their organization. Others establish diversity mentorship programs that pair a person of color with an executive within the organization. This might be paid or unpaid but offers the mentee valuable insight into the workings of the company and access to one of its best minds.

I recently worked with a client to set up quarterly events featuring the who's who of people of color. For example, I suggested inviting Washington's only Black Supreme Court justice to host an event where she would answer questions about her journey, talk about the process of becoming a judge, and offer advice to interested and eager legal professionals. My client would then reach out to the Black Bar Association, or other Black organizations that would benefit from learning from her. This would bridge more connections with Black students, younger attorneys and legal professionals who could then be considered for positions when they become available. Instead of having a mindset of "reaching out" to diverse communities of talent, try the approach of "attracting" them.

Others put their money where their mouths are by funding scholarships for people of color in high school to ensure they can attend the college of their choice and get access to top quality education.

Keeping an Eye on Equity

Establishing pay equity is one of the easiest and most effective tools organizations can use to ensure their commitment to equity is matched by their actions and communicates to their employees that a real change in corporate culture has occurred.

As part of their equity assessment, one of my clients conducted an audit and discovered that salaries were all over the map with no apparent rhyme or reason. In the end, several staff members ended up getting pay increases, all of them staff of color incidentally. One of these staff members ended up with a $12,000 annual increase.

Lastly, each company should reevaluate the company handbook to see if any of the policies listed within it represent quiet or overt racism. Ask questions like:

1. Does our organization have rules about hairstyles that disenfranchise Black women? One client had a "no dreadlocks" policy because it was "too distracting."
2. Does our organization support political initiatives that signal white supremacy, racism, or that lean toward political efforts that marginalize people from certain groups?
3. Does our organization have a clear, written and widely-communicated policy about how complaints will be handled?
4. What ongoing methods do we employ to ensure that changes that are made funnel completely from top to bottom and bottom to top?
5. Are we sure that changes that are made are communicated consistently from manager to manager?
6. Are our policies, practices and processes implemented consistently?

I had a client that allowed each manager to determine how they wanted to conduct their performance evaluations. In the leader's mind, she was allowing each manager to have freedom to create a process that worked best for their teams. As a result, some staff got very detailed and helpful feedback. Others, unfortunately, did not. The forms and tools used to conduct the evaluation were different among the managers. Some were cumbersome and difficult to complete, and others were easy and efficient. What was also problematic was the consistency of evaluations. Some received evaluations every year and others hadn't had one for a few years. Because evaluations were tied to merit increases, this left some without salary increases for years, while others got a bump in salary every year. These inconsistencies in practice and implementation produced inconsistent outcomes for staff.

Asking the Right Questions

Organizations can easily gauge the veracity of the claims to support diversity and inclusion by asking the right questions at every level of leadership within the company. The answers to these questions help to reveal motive as well as commitment to the values they claim to espouse.

Question #1 – Is our DEI initiative adding real value to people within our organization or in our customer or user base? If so, can we name the value-add in concrete terms and measure its impact?

It's easy to use acceptable corporate language about steps companies are taking to improve race relations. But often, those words are little more than noise. They have no real practical application beyond their placement on a website or on a corporate brochure. There is no receiver on the other end of their effort. So, the gift is hollow. What are the specific and measurable goals and metrics?

Question #2 – Would the message be just as effective if stated by a single individual as well as an organization? In other words, if it was said person-to-person, would it sound sincere or insincere?

For example, do the following DEI goals give you a clear sense of what the organization is actually doing?

- Engage all team members in meaningful dialogue.
- Heighten awareness of inclusive hiring practices.
- Revise the organization's values on anti-racism.

It is easy to see that these are nothing words and they will produce nothing results. They aren't specific. Instead, the organization might try:

- Host a catered diversity town hall once per month, inviting all stakeholders to share concerns and solutions in a safe and open forum.
- Adjust the hiring process to have candidates evaluated by a diverse committee rather than a single person.
- Implement a mentorship program that provides opportunities for people of color and fosters diversity.

These are the kinds of action items that can be implemented easily. Even if there was staff turnover, a new person could pick up these initiatives and run with them.

Question #3 – Is our DEI initiative a long-term commitment of the organization? If so, what steps have been put in place to ensure it lasts?

Organizations tend to be reactionary. They do what they see others do in response to whatever is happening at the moment in the culture. Real change is not transitory. It doesn't ebb and flow with public opinion. Diversity and inclusion are values that stand the test of time. Organizations that are simply trying to match the temperature of the culture will appear reactionary, phony, and/or unreliable. And their initiatives will pop like a firecracker and then fizzle into nothing. This often leaves staff, especially staff of color, deflated and demoralized feeling like their lived experiences and concerns are viewed as little more than a fad.

Question #4 – What cost are we willing to pay for our DEI initiative?

This is always where the rubber meets the road. We put our money where our values are. Organizations can make statements, issue press releases, and run ads all day long. However, the question that is begged is whether they are willing to lose profits, donors, or other financial incentives for taking a stand. Paying employees of color what they deserve costs money. Replacing staff who don't comply with company policy costs money. Providing time and space for discussion costs money. When companies are truly committed to diversity, they make the financial decision first. Organizations that won't make the financial sacrifice may just as well scrap the diversity talk altogether.

Question #5 - What is the value added to the people of color within the organization?

Real initiatives that are backed by commitment, led by the white community in the organization, sanctioned by people of color and financed by the organization will add real value to the lives of the people of color it is meant to serve. If it doesn't, it is little more than a campaign promise. Little more than noise.

Value adds result in partnerships, promotions, pay increases, mentorships, scholarships, morale boost, retention, collaboration between ethnicities, sharing of resources, and building of bridges between people. In other words, value adds create a buzz in the organization and heightens the excitement. Will everyone sign off on the changes? No. But, overall, there will be renewed energy.

Question #6 – Is our DEI initiative about public optics or about transforming our organization?

This doesn't mean that good decisions about equity won't create publicity for the organization. In fact, they will. But the intent of the initiative should not be related to verbiage on a brochure, press releases, or posts on the organization's website. It should be about meaningful change for those most impacted in the organization.

Question #7 - Are the Directors and Managers of the organization subject to our DEI initiative?

This is another place where a zero-sum game is the only option. The Director cannot demand that middle managers diversify while the Director keeps themselves in a bubble of white people-only. The Director must be the model of this work. Leadership by example is the only way to demonstrate true commitment to anti-racism. Also, there must be diverse voices and perspectives at the leadership table to weigh in on DEI within the organization.

Question #8 – Are we sensitive and aware of the nuances of anti-blackness?

People really struggle with anti-blackness — especially other people of color who often respond with, "What about *my* people?" I get it, and I do believe that white supremacy creates a "one microphone" phenomenon which means that we can't all have our trauma simultaneously. This leads people of color to believe that they can't support and uplift other races without it meaning that their own racial identity is somehow negated or dismissed. The reality is that we, as Black Americans, have to protest and argue just to say we matter.

The history of brutality toward black people and *Indigenous people* are very unique in our American story. Many, if not most, Black

Americans center their racial identities above their other identities. This is because it's not always obvious if you are gay, trans, living with a disability, Muslim, Christian, impoverished, or wealthy. But for the most part, it *is* obvious if you are Black. Just ask racist police officers what they see first.

Organizations must work to understand the deeply embedded structures that dehumanize and marginalize Black people in this country to better appreciate why your Black colleagues don't want to participate on DEI committees, refuse to speak up about issues they see, or they just adopt a "keep my head down, work, and go home" approach.

You will also be better able to see how other non-Black staff who don't respect these nuances will just think they are angry, or non-participatory.

With grace, it will be easier to embrace the realities that many Black folks are just tired and often fearful of letting their guards down.

Other tools organization can use to ensure they reach their goals are:

Diversity committees. DEI committees help to deepen analysis and can assist in developing an action plan.

Small group sessions. People are often more willing to speak freely in small groups rather than in a room filled with people. Create spaces that support these smaller sessions.

Caucus facilitation. Caucuses gather homogenous groups together to conference. Sometimes people are more open to sharing with others who are like them at first. This gives them a chance to "test share" with the group and process some of their thoughts and ideas before gathering in larger mixed sessions.

To have meaningful discussions about race, grace serves as the lens through which we evaluate our communications. One reason discussions of race are avoided or fail completely is because of the fear of a misstep. People might be silently wondering:

- What if I say the wrong thing?
- What if I offend someone?
- What if I don't use the right terminology?
- What if something I have always said has been deemed by the culture as inappropriate without my knowledge?
- What if I am not ready to surrender a belief I have long held?
- What if I change other people's favorable opinion of me?

These are the questions that bubble under the surface of conversations we have about race. And the fear of a misstep can outweigh any desire to resolve issues. People believe (sometimes rightly) that something they say will be held against them in a performance review or when collaborating with others. They wonder, if they share honestly, will they be welcome at the lunch table or invited to the pub for an after-work drink.

> *Tough conversations require openness, bravery, the ability to work through discomfort, express views in a non-combative manner, and to listen and reflect without judgment. People teams should consider the organizational culture, values and whether it has experience of having candid conversations and receiving feedback.*

> *Where open and constructive conversation is the norm, there's a strong likelihood that the organization is ready to have conversations about race. Reminding your employees about your values, principles and organizational approach of honesty and openness would be a great idea.*
>
> *Example: Our organizational values of compassionate honesty, looking after each other and listening to understand will support us all as we share and learn about each other's experience of race.* (Chartered Institute of Personnel and Development , 2022)

If an organization does not already enjoy a culture of openness in conversation, it is not going to be easy to establish such a culture on the issue of race equity. Many organizations, in fact, operate on precisely the opposite paradigm. People are afraid to speak freely or are always navigating the politics around what they say. And if they have ever experienced retaliation formally or informally, they will not be likely to venture into the deep again. This is where an outside consultation or a facilitator can be helpful. This person's job is to assure every participant that they are not obligated to get it right and that they are free to share without any fear of retribution from the organization.

Resistance is inevitable. So, the conversation of grace must permeate all conversations and actions. Each person should embrace his or her own vulnerability and celebrate the vulnerability of others. This will help each person to shed their fears and take yet another step toward the others in the community. When the walls of fear, self-protection, and judgment are torn down and participants stand under grace, they become emotionally accessible to the others in the group. They are able to challenge their beliefs and make measurable changes in behavior.

Don't let perfection be the enemy of vulnerability (in terms of not being silent because you're afraid to mess up).

Finally, age can sometimes play a major role in this process. While this is not true across the board, people who are older may find it hard to surrender their generational norms and standards for new paradigms. To them, it may feel like a merry-go-round that never stops and lets them get off or, at least, catch their breath. I have witnessed the impatience and judgment by younger folks for whom the new terminology, technology, and perspectives are natural. I call for an abundance of patience and grace as our older colleagues challenge years of programming and are (in many cases) genuinely trying to adopt these new ways to think about the world.

CHAPTER 8 – I AM THE WORK

The fact is, racism is reflected in every institution and organization in the U.S.: social change groups are not exempt. The structures and cultures of community-based, grassroots groups reproduce the white privilege and racial oppression of the wider society. Whatever your social change mission, it's bound to fall short as long as racism continues to flourish and maintain the status quo. (Western States Center, 2001)

We've talked about what it takes to steer the ship of organizations large and small, and that they don't move easily or fast. But what does it take to chart a new course on a personal level?

Individual responsibility is as important to the nature of the organization's culture as the larger perspective of a big machine. Each person must engage in the kind of self-reflection that produces inner change — change that is long-lasting and visible to all.

Self-reflection is the cornerstone of grace. If you can't extend grace to yourself, it is difficult to extend grace to others. This is a time when you must love yourself enough to give yourself the grace you need to be open and merciful. Only then can you do the same for others. I have a friend named Rhona and every time someone would get uptight, hostile, or frustrated, she would say, "Grace and mercy, friend… grace and mercy." When I thought of my neighbor who approached me, I was later calm enough to take deep breaths and say, "Grace and mercy, Michelle." What if in his most honest attempt, that was the only way he knew how to connect with me? What if he was genuinely trying to thank me for causing his breakthrough on how he saw the world? What if that breakthrough changed how he treated his employees, or students, or coworkers? Grace and mercy.

At the same time, as the person on the receiving end of his breakthrough, all I can do is the best I can do. Grace and mercy must extend to oneself as well.

While the ability to self-reflect in real time is powerful for changing outcomes in the moment, that isn't always possible. However, there is still tremendous power in critically looking back over our past decisions and behaviors to understand the different levers and triggers that provoke our responses. Only then, can we do something differently next time.

What's in your wagon?

In my trainings, I use the example of the *Little Red Wagon of Issues*. This is a concept that describes all of the wounds, judgments and beliefs we walk through life with. We all walk around with our little red wagon of issues. They are with us. Many of us don't know what's in our wagon, or that we even have one at all. Our wagon issues manifest themselves in ways that we aren't often unaware of. I'll give you two examples from my own life.

Wagon issue #1 - I mentioned that I grew up in conditions of homelessness. For so long during this time, I was never able to make decisions for myself. I was forced to endure situations in which my voice was taken from me. I never felt safe and secure, which is an essential human need, especially for a child. I was always living under someone else's rules, values, and attitudes. I was always told what to do and what to think. I vowed that one day no one will EVER tell me what to do. As a result, to this day, I am *ferociously* protective of my agency, voice, and ability to make my own choices. If I in *any way* feel micromanaged, forced, or told what to do, I get anxious and angry. Like, immediately. Every time. This is what's in my wagon. It goes with me everywhere.

Wagon issue #2 - My mother used to be obsessed with time and lateness. For as long as I can remember, she would tell me "Time is the most precious thing you have. If people don't respect your time, they don't respect you. Period." So, of course, I adopted that as a belief. Luckily for me, I've had plenty of opportunities to work through this issue with a husband who is chronically late, but it was a bumpy road in the beginning of our relationship.

But I do have a wagon issue about people being late. This meant that whenever someone was late, I was automatically pissed off and couldn't move past it. I literally couldn't hear them because... how and why should I listen to a person who doesn't respect me?

Interacting vs. Inner-acting

So how do my wagon issues play out? I remember my manager asking me clarifying questions about a presentation I was preparing to give. She gave some great feedback and suggestions, but all I heard was criticism and micromanagement. I snapped at her (wearing a smile, of course) with that Seattle *nicey-nice* passive aggressiveness: "So it seems like you have an idea of how you want this to look. Would you like to do it?"

She snapped back startlingly loud, "Wow! Where is this coming from?"
I said, "I need to breathe for a minute."

She clapped back at me, "Yeah... you do."

So, I walked out and took a breath.

Here we go! My wagon issues were coming on full force without my consent or control. They were just... there. And I was furious. *Why even ask me to do it if you wanted to do it? You don't trust me? Why are you telling me what to do?*

When we finally resumed our conversation, I was a bit more calm but still angry. As we talked more and she began to share, what surfaced is her deep-seated wagon issues about people disregarding her input and voice. She was the youngest of five children and always felt like no one took her seriously. She vowed that she would be the boss so that people *had* to listen to her. She, too, was angry. For her, what I was essentially saying was "Your voice doesn't matter. You don't matter. I'm listening to you."

And so it goes. Two people who have genuine respect and care for one another, have all but disappeared and our wagons are violently banging against each other.

We thought we were "interacting" but truly we were "*inner-acting*." Our inner wounds and securities took over and we became merely bystanders.

Identifying *what's* in your wagon is the beginning of owning your issues, as opposed to them owning you. Grace begins with being able to own your *total* self.

Still, some people will struggle and may need the support of the team to dive deeper into their thoughts and feelings. The more people who they see doing this deep work, the more likely that the people who struggle will feel safe to do so as well. This, again, is an expression of grace as we assist people in the hard work — *the heart work* — of owning their emotions and behaviors around race. We should be careful not to assume that, just because a person is older, they are hardened on race and, just because a person is young, they are open and accepting. Race and racism mean different things to different people of all ages. And, similarly, grace will mean different things to them as well.

What Grace Means for People of Color

Grace for people of color begins by a simple acknowledgement that the world has established a system where people of color have a harder time in business, housing, human relationships, law enforcement encounters, and every other area of life.

Many white people, in an attempt to escape the sins of their forefathers and foremothers, try to wash their hands of racism as an issue altogether. They consider a conversation with them about race as "preaching to the choir" and believe that they can understand what it means to live in a world that is systemically skewed against people of color. This perspective poisons the conversation and restores the anger and resentment we sought to quell with grace.

Ignoring race, rejecting the presence of racism, pretending it doesn't exist in one's own heart, and making comments about the rainbow of colors (I don't care if someone is blue, purple, pink, or green) only exacerbates a topic that is fraught with misgivings. Since there are no purple people, the comment has the opposite of its intended effect and only frustrates efforts to bring the races together.

Grace equity must extend to people of color in the simple acknowledgement that they exist in the context of a racist system.

In a practical sense, here are few things to consider as we consider grace for people of color.

- If you are conducting an "implicit bias" training, for example, give people of color the option to opt out as most of these training center around white people and the behavior *they* need to change.

- When 230 Indigenous children are found in a mass grave, your Indigenous staff will have a different world to live in that day - one filled with grief and/or anger. When a Black man is killed by police, know that Black people in your organization are going to have a *different* day as well as they are overwhelmed with emotions.

- When a Black colleague reacts to something that is said or done in the organization or in conversation, take the posture of a student. Ask questions and prepare your heart and mind to learn.

- If a Black woman elevates her voice, she could be hurt, excited, passionate, or frustrated. But she should never be assumed to be angry by those who are threatened by Black women expressing emotion. If she is angry, consider the circumstances and environment that generated this anger, as opposed to just her tone of voice. Listen to her words!

I want to be sensitive to people of color reading this. It may feel that these are not acts of grace, but instead acts of humanity. It should be obvious right? For example, Instead of Implicit Bias, what if your organization were conducting a training on rape culture? Would we require women who were impacted or traumatized by rape attend that training? This is only retraumatizing. Same with people who have been traumatized by racism. To make them sit in a space with people who are a part of the system that perpetuates their harm does nothing but generate pain and frustration.

What Grace Means for Black and Indigenous People

To be clear, Black and Indigenous people in this country have had a *vastly* different experience from other racial groups. If we go back to their origins, the murder, physical abuse, and psychological torture of African and Indigenous people were purposeful and capitalistic in nature. When someone comes into your home, slaughters half the people in your house, and sends the rest to the basement to live, just so they can profit from your home, they will go to great lengths to ensure that the people in the basement remain invisible. And that is what we see today. Our Indigenous brothers and sisters are invisible *and invisibilized* in our political, social, and financial systems.

If the captors then go down the street and kidnap a group of people from their homes to upkeep this stolen house, a different strategy becomes necessary. These new captives cannot simply be killed and put away because the captors need them. They will need to figure out a way to subjugate people's physical bodies *against their will*. First, they would need to take away everything that gives this group its power. Their names, their spirituality, their families, their history and, of course, their freedom. Then the captors would need to ensure that the captives adopt and self-perpetuate *their* beliefs, values, spirituality and systemic arrangement of oppression. This is what we see today in the internalized hatred against other Black people: little to no connection with African heritage, loss of spirituality and power, and gatekeeping against their own best interests.

For sure, other groups experience racism and oppression. However, Black and Indigenous oppression is built and sustained for one purpose—*wealth of white men*. This is the fundamental difference.

Black and Indigenous people need grace. When they are sharing their experiences, resist the urge to say, "My struggle, my people, or my voice is being silenced". Or compare your struggle to theirs. We all have our unique challenges in this country. But the way toward healing is to listen to, and understand the differences between *all* of us, without it meaning anything about you.

On a final note, if you want to be gracious you have to understand the ways in which your beliefs are counter to grace.

As best-selling author Robin DiAngelo wrote:

> *"A white participant said... "I don't see race; I don't see you as black." My co-trainer's response was, "Then how will you see racism?" He then explained to her that he was black, he was confident that she could see this, and that his race meant that he had a very different experience in life than she did. If she were ever going to understand or challenge racism, she would need to acknowledge this difference. Pretending that she did not notice that he was black was not helpful to him in any way, as it denied his reality – indeed, it refused his reality – and kept hers insular and unchallenged. This pretense that she did not notice his race assumed that he was "just like her," and in so doing, she projected her reality onto him. For example, I feel welcome at work so you must too; I have never felt that my race mattered, so you must feel that yours doesn't either. But of course, we do see the race of other people, and race holds deep social meaning for us."*
> *— Robin DiAngelo, White Fragility: Why It's So Hard for White People to Talk About Racism*

Leaders of Color

There will be some challenging times as a leader of color. One of my clients is a Black woman. I have witnessed firsthand how people challenge her every decision. She is one of the most transparent, vulnerable, and transformational leaders I've ever worked with. Most of the major decisions she makes come with an opportunity for staff to ask questions and provide feedback. She has increased salaries across the board to ensure equity. She has an open-door policy that allows for anyone on staff to access her directly. I could go on about her efforts to make sure that everyone on staff feels seen and heard. Every. Single. One.

Yet... I've *never* seen any leader more scrutinized about their decisions than her. I've joked that if she walked on water, people would say that she's just hiding the fact that she can't swim.

Enter grace. This leader and other leaders of color will find their greatest power in understanding that people fear what they are not used to. Also, people are often guided by their implicit biases. So, they may not even realize that they are being more judgmental or harsh in their perceptions of the leader of color. Here are some other dynamics that leaders of color often face:

- **Anti-Blackness.** I had a conversation with a staff member who identified as Asian and said, "I just get mad that every time we talk about race, it has to be centered around Blacks. What about us? Asian lives matter, too." As I stated in the previous chapter, systemic racism sets up the "one Mic" scenario. If we are talking about Black Policing, we can't talk about anti-Asian hate. If we are talking about issues related to Trans folks, we can't talk about immigration and farm worker protections. We have to be sensitive to everyone's lived experiences. Grace is seeing someone else's pain just as real and relevant as our pain is to us. We cannot conflate the issue by mixing in other societal ills. Each one deserves our focused attention.

- **Internalized Racism.** In reference to the leader I mentioned, I was shocked when I saw the distrust and disrespect by folks of color. White supremacy has people of color buy-in to their narrative of *white as right*. So as people try to fit in and be successful, they ascribe to white supremacy norms, which means people of color will turn on each other. This is part of the system, and the only thing that changes people's minds and hearts is direct experience, or stories that connect someone to a direct experience. So, as a leader of color, we must keep on keepin' on in grace with a right mind and heart and hope people will catch on.

- **Managing Staff of Color.** I see leaders of color who give staff of color a pass because they figure that life is hard enough. If they don't turn in that report on time, they give grace, recognizing the harsh realities of our world are harsher for people of color. This is a slippery slope because their work can impair another person's work. Also, at what point is this person's growth being stifled by lowering the bar of expectation?

  o Conversely, I've seen the reverse where leaders of color are harder on staff of color to toughen them and set them up for preparation for this cruel racist world. Either way, if we can just realize that both of these leaders are reacting to racism. Therefore, in their attempt to support staff who are harmed by racism, they often under-correct or over-correct, using the racist tactics of under-correction and overcorrection.

- **Managing White Staff.** Finally, as a Leader of Color, it's quite possible that you have white staff that you lead. I've seen:
    - White staff who sabotage leaders of color
    - White staff who, as allies, lift leaders of color up, and other allies who, in their efforts to show allyship, say or do things that end up harming or undermining the leader of color.
    - White staff who feel emboldened to tell the leader how to do their job.
    - White staff who publicly call out the leader of color in a way that is meant to humiliate and embarrass.
    - I've seen one leader of color announce to her staff that she was leaving and some of the white staff shamed and guilted her, as one stated, "I thought we were a family? Is this new opportunity really worth it?"

Indeed, leading as a person can often be a heavy lift. All of the above experiences are based out of fear, and the wounds and insecurities from people's little red wagon. The leader must use the tools of self-reflection and grace to meet these challenges head on.

What Grace Means for White People

Grace for white people will take on many forms. For starters, grace compels us to accept that the benefits white people receive from racism come to them without their active participation. No white person is born knowing that they have an advantage. They come to this understanding over time. Depending on who raised them and what factors influence them, they will acknowledge or refuse to acknowledge those advantages.

But grace begs the question: What then is a white person to do about the privileges racism has bought for them? White people cannot be punished for the system that catered to their skin color for the duration of their lives. Can they?

White people are tasked with understanding that the issue of racism is a fundamentally "white problem." Since people of color are on the receiving end of racism, they lack the power to effect change outside of calling attention to it wherever it rears its ugly head. But white people have the ability to crush racism in their own hearts and in the organizations where they work, serve, and play.

That said, I believe that grace should also be extended to those white people *who are alongside us in the fight.* Doing the difficult work of erasing the stain of racism and constantly battling other white folks in the name of justice for all is no easy task and requires consistent soul-searching by white folks. They must also do the work of defining for themselves what it means to be responsible for and accountable to the grace extended to them.

Also, we must find a way to hold safe spaces for authentic conversations. As a Black woman who does this work, I am all too aware of the many questions that some white people ask that, for me, seem painfully obvious. Sometimes the questions seem so loud I feel my ears ringing, my legs turn to jelly, and my hands begin to shake.

"Dr. Majors," said one training participant, "Do Black people ever come together and talk about how far we've come as a nation. Ya know, like, we can all use the same bathroom and drink out of the same water faucet. There has been some progress made, right?"

Here was my reply. "Let's say your internet goes down, you have a very important zoom call in 10 minutes. You frantically call your internet provider's customer care and quickly tell them that your internet is down. As you try to explain how urgent and important it is to get your internet back up immediately, the customer care person interrupts you and says, 'Hey slow down, we used to have dial up that took five minutes to connect and worked at a fraction of the speed. Rather than being mad about your internet being down, look how far internet technology has come. Remember that screeching sound every time you would try to connect? I mean we've come so far. Do you ever just sit and ponder how far we've come since dial up?'"

The flurry of private chats I received in real time was my indicator that the point was made.

I then explained that two things didn't happen on that call with the customer care agent:

1. Your needs still didn't get met.
2. The agent never even acknowledged your sense of urgency.

So much of the frustration as a person of color is that it feels like people don't understand or acknowledge your pain, and they don't change or do anything to change the circumstances that generate that pain. Police are still killing Black people, and it is often explained away by the very people charged with eradicating such cultural evils. When politicians, police chiefs, and other community leaders fail to act with urgency, it only exacerbates the pain.

With all of this, there is still a very real need for white people to be able to ask these questions and hear the answers. Designated spaces where people of color and white people can listen and hear one another. This will take grace for people of color to engage with white people without getting so triggered that they shut down. Of course, there are limitations, and no one should be disrespected, but as long as there is an earnest agreement that we count these kinds of questions to one's head and not their heart, I believe we can somehow push through to dialogue that brings us together and not tear us apart. We have to figure this out and offer grace to people who are still evolving.

Racism is ubiquitous, it can be mentally and emotionally exhausting to be vigilant about interrupting racism everywhere we see it. Grace extends to those white people in their struggle as they take up the mantle for the common goal of oneness.

White Leaders

White leaders have an especially challenging task. As the people with systemic and organizational power, they must be vigilant about how to address, on a personal level, the racism they have allowed as a white person and as an organizational leader. They must be courageous.

To be clear, it takes a tremendous amount of courage to be a white ally while also being a leader. While both people of color and some white folks will say, "Cry me a river; it may be hard to be courageous, but it's even harder to be oppressed." Perhaps, but on a personal level, none of that matters in the moment when you have to make those difficult decisions to call people out, confront your own biases, or admit some mistakes that you know will make things worse before they get better.

Following are a few points of reflection that may help white leaders in their journey towards leading with grace:

- **Do your work.** By this I mean, be clear about what is in your little red wagon that can get in the way of your ability to be vulnerable and courageous. You will have to figure out how to have grace for yourself, first.

- **Get your definitions clear.** Define what grace means *to* you, what grace means *for* you and what it looks like for your staff. This is an excellent exercise to do with your leadership team. "What does grace mean for our team? What would that look like? How do we model grace in our organization? How do we model grace for each other as leaders? How do we cultivate a culture where people can take risks and make mistakes, knowing that we center grace and restoration when mistakes are made? Be relentless in your pursuit of ensuring grace is present in every aspect of your organization from performance reviews to conflict management to termination of employees.

- **Become a master listener.** Recognize that as a white leader, you must develop ultra-listening skills because you can never know racism like people of color do. So, listen and take what your staff of color tell you seriously. People of color often don't feel heard or believed. They are often required to prove their position. Demonstrate that everyone is heard and given the benefit of the doubt. Then make decisions from there.

- **Be transparent.** People of color have had a tragic history in this country and are understandably skeptical. So, to mitigate distrust with your staff of color, more transparency is better. As much as you can share appropriately, will go a long way in people understanding your thought process and values.

- **Connect with people human to human.** Talk to people about regular human things. As much as you can or are willing to share, let people know some of your story. When people know your story, they can better know you and feel more connected.

- **Call things out and DO NOT let known issues fester**. Too many times to count, I have seen prevalent issues in an organization that have gone on for so long that people assume one of three things: 1) leadership is onboard with the issue or behavior, 2) leadership doesn't see it or 3) leadership doesn't care. None of these are good.

- **If you manage staff of color, it is important to trust their skills and brilliance**. Expect them to be successful, give them the tools to do so, and step aside. Make sure that they know they can admit their mistakes and together you will restore things. But above all, don't be afraid of your staff of color, especially Black staff. People don't want to admit that they are afraid of Black people, which is why I often find myself coaching white leaders on how to performance manage Black staff because the leader is often afraid to. Our tone, expressions, and directness are often weaponized against us.
    - When leaders are undergoing a race equity movement, they are more sensitive to the ways in which Black people are oppressed, so they are likely to be more afraid of performance management, so as to not burden them even more.
    - Conversely, leaders who are not intentional about bringing race equity to their organizations lean the opposite way. They tend to be harsher and more punitive of their Black staff and have no reservations about over managing them.

Holding People Big and Small

When I lived in NYC, I experienced a horrible breakup. I had moved from Chicago to New York to be with a man who had been my best friend for seven years. We both figured, "Hey, aren't you supposed to marry your best friend? Plus, if things don't work out, we can always just go back to friendship." Well, after I got there, we both soon realized that it was a huge, HUGE mistake. In the end, I had lost my boyfriend and the one person I would typically turn to. My best friend was now also gone. I was alone in New York, and I was a wreck.

While going through the pain of this breakup, my good friend, Pat, was coming from Chicago to New York to see the *Color Purple* and asked if I wanted to join her.

Now, before I continue, I have to tell you a little about Pat Perkins. Pat is a coach. But she's not an ordinary coach. She is what you call "a velvet hammer." She will give it to you straight with directness and grace. She has very little patience with self-pity or self-deprecation. With Pat, you walk in with a break down, you walk out with a breakthrough. That's it. That's all.

So, Pat came to New York. Knowing that I was in breakdown and couldn't pull myself out of my anger and pity, our mutual friend, Cecilia, said, "This is perfect! Pat will be there, and she can help you move past this."

My immediate response was, "I can't ask Pat for help." Cecilia was perplexed and asked me to explain. I replied, "Pat is not the space for bullshit."

Cecilia knew exactly what I was talking about. What we both knew was that, unless you are ready to do the work, don't bother Pat. And even though I said I was, I knew I wasn't. I was still feeling small and was committed to my story about being a victim. I saw myself as small, and I knew Pat would see me too big to validate this "woe is me" narrative. Pat ain't havin' none of it. So, there is no way that I would bring it to her.

You see, Pat is someone who holds people accountable to their bigness, even when they see themselves as small. In other words, she holds them *big*. I can't tell you how uncomfortable it is to be in the presence of someone who sees your greatness while you are actively refusing to rise to it. This is what makes Pat both brilliant and terrifying.

How do you hold your staff? If you hold them big you will:
- Relate to them as capable thought partners who are able to hear your feedback and make the necessary adjustments to shine.
- Give them direct feedback without a lot of mental rehearsal of what you will say and how you think they can handle it.
- Balance accountability and grace and say the difficult things, then ask them if they have any questions or concerns, giving them space to react and respond. And, because you know that they are working through their own thing, you trust that they will sort themselves out and be fine.

If you hold your people small you will:
- Micromanage the hell out of them because you don't trust them to perform.
- Coddle them – This will look like giving people what they want so they don't feel bad or spending a lot of time managing staff emotions rather than allowing people to have their emotions and letting them know your door is open when they are ready to have a restorative conversation.
- Plan out exactly how to give critical or constructive feedback in a way that doesn't hurt their feelings, or make them feel bad, knowing that they will be too fragile to hear it.

- Hold back on doing and saying many things because you don't want to appear racist. Or if you are a person of color, you will do everything in your power to avoid looking like the angry rebel rouser.

Other instances I've seen of holding people small in a racialized context:

- Black leaders that manage Black staff and don't hold them accountable for mistakes because, "It's hard being Black, I don't want to put more of a burden on them."
- Black leaders who push Black staff too hard because, "I need to be harder on them so they can be ten times better than their white counterparts."
- White leaders who refuse to give critical feedback or performance manage staff of color because they don't want to be called racist.
- White men who give breaks to other white men because, "It's open season on white straight men, and it's important that he has a safe place... (to say inappropriate things)."
- Leaders who give a pass to more senior staff and don't require them to engage in DEI work because, "They are old dogs and it's not fair to expect them to learn new tricks at this point in their career."
- Leaders who do the work cover up or cleanup for non-performing staff, rather than require them to do their work.

All of this is about choosing to honor and respect your staff's brilliance and let them shine. Of course, there are folks, like I was, who can't see their own bigness and act out in small ways that harm the organization. This is a completely different dynamic and needs attention immediately.

The final and most important aspect of holding people *big* is related to the bigness of the leader. As a leader, there is no way to give feedback, hold people accountable, performance manage, or create trust when you don't see yourself as big. It can feel scary to have to do things that will make people feel angry, sad, scared, or defensive. This is why it is so important for each leader reading this to do his or her work.

Confront your own anger, sadness, fear, or defensiveness and accept it as a human experience. Then you will be able to see it in another with grace and compassion instead of fear.

People leading the difficult work of grace equity are blazing new trails. They are learning and will likely make mistakes along the way. Grace teaches us to prepare for those mistakes, and be so accepting of ourselves, that we are not crushed under the pressure of looking perfect or getting it right. This work has no place for perfection. Leading with grace is all about how we stand back up and restore ourselves and each other after we've fallen down.

A point we covered earlier bears repeating here. In a post-pandemic world, the atmosphere is ripe for a movement of grace equity. It's easy to be self-focused when all is well in the world. But, having stared down death, having seen corpses piled high in the U. S. and abroad, having lived for nearly two years in isolation, I believe that people are more open to breaking down the barriers that had been erected in their lives since birth. This is work we must do together no matter where we land in the conversation. We must all own our part. While Black people might be reticent about being engaged after years of trying to bring about change, ultimately, with true grace, mercy, and a commitment toward change, even the latecomers will come around and join the effort.

CHAPTER 9 – G.R.A.C.E. IS

"The function, the very serious function of racism is distraction. It keeps you from doing your work. It keeps you explaining, over and over again, your reason for being. Somebody says you have no language and you spend twenty years proving that you do. Somebody says your head isn't shaped properly so you have scientists working on the fact that it is. Somebody says you have no art, so you dredge that up. Somebody says you have no kingdoms, so you dredge that up. None of this is necessary. There will always be one more thing."
— *Toni Morrison*

G

Growth mindset
It has been said that there are two major mindsets: a growth mindset and a fixed mindset. People who are fixed on the issue of race are not willing to change any facet of their inner ideology. To develop a growth mindset, one needs to be a continual learner. The landscape is changing and we must keep our minds open to new ways to think and understand the world and others around us.

More and more, I am seeing clashes as a result of generational differences in which the quickly changing landscape is making it more difficult for us to speak the same language. People who are older may feel forced to make changes when those changes come too fast for them to keep up. And younger people may grow impatient with people who don't jump on board every cultural shift. It is important for both young and older folks to have a growth mindset. None of us have arrived, and each of us has more to learn.

Get some space
Separate yourself from the issue so that you can think clearly. Sometimes things are just heated and you can only access grace when you step away and reflect.

R

Reconciliation
Past organizational harms leave scars on the people who were affected by those harms. However, people who witnessed the wrongdoing are also impacted by harms perpetrated on others, even when the witness suffered no losses at all.

What happens when you watch an injustice occur and do nothing to address it? I believe that a piece of your soul is lost when you deny the humanity of others. You are fundamentally changed by your own inaction and must, now, reclaim your conscience.

Relationships
We give more grace to those we are in relationships with. Relationships are built on knowing another's story. There is no substitute for knowing another person's story. It takes them from a stereotype to an individual. When we know each other's stories, we are able to understand how or why we think what we think.

Until then, suffice it to say, Grace makes relationships possible between people with profound differences. Only through relationships can people *truly* come to know each other and bond with those who differ from them.

Building meaningful relationships at work is more important than a lot of people will admit. The social dynamics at work become even more essential when you are doing race equity work which is fraught with tension and discomfort. I can say that some of my former coworkers were my friends and afforded me grace when I made mistakes... because they cared about me on a personal level.

Repairing and restoring
It's important to repair harm that is done. Think about times when people want to move past the harm without taking the time to repair and restore those they have hurt to a state of wholeness. It feels hard to move forward and they remain stuck in harm. Until people feel the harm is acknowledged and repaired and they are restored, then moving forward is hindered.

Respect
This can be a loaded term, as the word "respect" is weaponized to mean "respect my authority." But, in grace equity, we do not toss around our titles, seniority, experience, or any other accolades. We are all completely equal. In essence, it's respect for a person's humanity and dignity. Respect brings with it and experience of being fully seen and known.

Releasing the old
Organizations learn to let go of the dreaded seven words, "That's the way it's always been done." Defaulting to unchallenged norms that have been historically harmful.

Resilience
Humans bounce back! We do! We get knocked down, but we get back up again. We rise and fall. We try, fail, and try again. Grace provides the space to keep coming back to the table and give it

another shot. To try again to understand. To ask for something to be explained again. To tell your story one more time.

A

Accountability
The other side to the Grace coin is accountability. Grace with no accountability doesn't allow for things to change. Accountability with no grace leads to people feeling guilty, shamed and unable to change their hearts.

Acknowledgment
It can also represent acknowledgment – part of what is happening in this country is that there has been no national recognition of the harms of slavery and the resulting years of segregation and Jim Crow. What happens in organizations is that there is no recognition of past harms that have been caused by unfair structural and cultural norms and then leaders want to hop straight into DEI work in order to "just move forward." Pushing past the pain does nothing to stop the pain.

Avoid Assumptions
We all make them. We make assumptions about what people mean, what they intended, how they felt, what they believe, and who they are. How do we understand and challenge our assumptions about others? Do we drive our assumptions or do our assumptions drive us? Why do we accept the assumptions we accept without question? If those assumptions fell, would our world view then change? If we are to truly change our organizations, and our world for that matter, it starts with us recognize the truth that we make many assumptions we make about one another and often these assumptions are intentionally established so that we remain divided and fearful of one another

Allow and own Anger
Anger is typically the most accessible and acceptable emotion (before hurt, or disappointment). I believe that people mask their embarrassment, shame, guilt, fear, sadness and even loneliness with anger. Grace gives us the space to name our anger. How do we understand and give room to our anger in a way that moves the conversation forward?

Authenticity
Learning to be yourself is the gift that keeps on giving. We often conform to what people want us to be. How can we be true to ourselves? Creating spaces of grace where we can have real conversations of vulnerability and truth allow us to be our authentic selves.

C

Courage
Courage must be at the foundation of any organization seeking grace equity. Courage to face one's own inner thoughts, courage to hear the concerns of others, courage to be right, courage to be wrong, and it takes courage to do the unfamiliar in pursuit of the highest ideals.

Does this all sound rather close to impossible — learning to extend (and receive) grace in our organizational conversations in ways that promote healing? That is because it is. Shifting one's own thought process, instincts, reflexes, habits, and attitudes is like turning a large ship in the ocean. It is difficult to move the heavy ballast of inequity. But that does not mean we can abdicate our responsibility to do so. What is hardest is often most necessary.

It takes courage to transform an organization into one that is healthy and whole where all members of the system feel safe to communicate with others openly. But without a clear vision and values, an organization is hardly an organism that can be expected to survive. It will eventually wither and die, the result of being starved of energy and vitality.

It takes courage to do this work and to be that one who names the thing that everyone sees, and does nothing about. As white leaders and leaders of color, we must develop the power that comes from courage and grace to lead organizations.

Collaboration

Once we are able to see each other, a new world opens up to us. We gain access to the insight and experiences others can offer. Collaboration is working together to get this done. It takes those with power working side-by-side with those without power.

One startup CEO wrote on a forum that he insisted on having maximum diversity at every planning meeting. His customers came in all shapes and sizes, so he demanded the same of his team. He noted that the best way to determine diversity at a meeting is to look under the table at the shoes of the attendees. If they are all the same — where it's all wingtips or all Birkenstocks, all high heels or all sneakers — adjourn the meeting, regroup, and start over.

Consistency

This is a marathon not a sprint. Real change takes consistency… over time. Never stop, just keep going and going and going. Part of what builds trust is an unwavering consistent message. I have seen leaders change course when things get rough. But these tough times are when it is most important to stay focused and consistent toward the vision.

Centering

We need to be able to be open and honest about centering race in our work. There are other oppressions, yes, but race is the ultimate form of oppression due to the nature of its very inception. No other "ism" was strategically designed for the sake of making and keeping white men rich. No other system has inherently built mechanisms for its self-perpetuation like racism. If we defeat racism, "other-ism" will too be defeated.

Curiosity

Stay curious about humanity, and you will be shocked, surprised, horrified, or delighted at what you learn. Don't ever stop wondering. Think about why people are so different. Do so without preconceived notions that any one group is superior to or inferior to another.

Clarity

We need to be clear about the vision and values of DEI work. Clarity gives us direction and purpose. It ensures we are all rowing in the same direction and heading for the same shore! Leadership must be crystal clear, because when the seas get rough, it will be easier to abandon ship. But if the destination is clear and compelling, we are more committed to the journey.

Challenge

Challenge your beliefs; challenge those who are causing disruptions in the culture; challenge norms. So much of the work is about changing people's behavior and very little is about changing *beliefs*. When grace is present, the more likely beliefs change, and behavior follows.

Commitment

You have to really be committed to this work. It is difficult and, if you are not grounded in a deep strong commitment, you will want to walk away. There will be rough patches. What will you do when the journey gets bumpy? Without commitment, you will quit.

E

Evolution
While I believe that revolutions have changed our world in powerful ways, I also believe that evolution eclipses revolution as minds become freed. Revolutions bring change fast through drastic measures. Evolutions take longer. Taking the red pill doesn't mean you open your eyes and find yourself in the promised land. Once a racist mind has been set free, they have a whole new reality to address. Everything they have known, believed, and relied on disappears in an instant, and they must learn how to navigate the new world. Organizations are often liberated one mind at a time. This is a slower process, which is why it is critical for leaders to do their own inner work related to racism so they are set up with the endurance, clarity, focus and grace for the long haul.

Empathy
We all need to learn how to tap into our stores of empathy. This is especially true for White people who have systemic power to invoke harm if they don't. This is a skill that we as humans have innately, but rarely use as a tool for effective communication. Empathy is the ability to place oneself in the position of someone else. But it doesn't stop there; once in that other person's position, one must be able to feel the feelings that align with that person's experience. Therein lies the catalyst for change. "If I were you, I would feel that way too" is one of the most powerful phrases one human being could offer another.

This evolution from surface empathy to deep empathy is what M. A. Clark and M. M. Young (Clark, Robertson, & Young, 2019) described in their paper on organizational empathy. They

124

described the progression from affective empathy (caring about how others feel) to cognitive empathy (caring what others think) to the holy grail of behavior empathy (behaving in a way that demonstrates empathy).

Examine your environment

How does your environment inform what you see and you HOW you see the world? What does your environment breed? Anxiety, overwork, competition? Or free-flowing ideas, collaboration, and celebration of the successes of others? This is one place that organizations can begin their work to shift their culture.

Embrace new possibilities

In addition, E can indicate our need to embrace new possibilities. Reimagine how your organization could look if everyone felt seen and felt that they belonged. The reality of grace equity is that it benefits everyone who embraces it. The victim is freed from the burden of their ethnicity or other marginalized identity. The perpetrator is liberated from a closed, fixed mindset that has kept them imprisoned, and the organization gains a new level of possible collaboration, mentorship, and growth among its members.

Imagine an organization where equity is held as one of the company's highest ideals. Meetings are refreshed by the air of grace extended to all staff alike. There is no sense of inferiority or superiority. As such, people are open and collaborative. They are willing to volunteer their ideas or offer to work on important projects. Innovative thought is freed because of the culture that encourages it. Each member of the team will do what they can to help others, seeing their efforts as part of the team's larger vision. The organization benefits. Individuals feel gratified in their work.

CHAPTER 10 – BRINGING GRACE TO ORGANIZATIONAL CONFLICT

Perhaps the most difficult, yet necessary place to apply grace is to conflict. Even when race is not involved, grace in a conflict helps to bring resolution to tense situations. When the powder keg of race comes close to the flame of conflict, grace is available to douse the pending explosion.

Conflict will always be present at the individual and organizational levels. While it may be unavoidable, it *is* manageable. Better said, it *must* be managed. Companies cannot afford to allow conflicts and the undercurrent of tension to dampen morale, cause outbursts, or cost the company quality employees. The financial burden of neglecting conflict can be extremely heavy. This is true for all organizations. And for nonprofit leaders who are often hyper-vigilant about every penny, the price of unresolved conflict is even more taxing.

In the previous chapter I discussed little red wagon issues. I talked about these issues in terms of wounds and trauma. But in this chapter, I will discuss wagon issues in terms of values and identity. We all hold sacred values that are important to us. For example, how I value autonomy and agency as a result of my wagon issues related to homelessness. These values anchor our world view, our interactions, and how we manage conflict. We also go through life with a particular identity that defines us. It's what we display to the world. The role of this identity is to protect the insecure, fearful, and angry child in all of us. But that's another book. We protect this identity at all costs and any threat that comes upon this identity we wage war with.

In my experience, at the heart of many, if not most conflicts are one of these two things, or both.

1. You feel your sacred values have been breached.
2. You feel your identity is threatened.

I will explain more in this story about a conflict I recently had.

I had a conflict with a white female colleague. I considered her a friend. She is an amazing person. She is a kind, sensitive and caring person who possessed a spot-on racial analysis that made her great to work with. Also, she kind of nerded-out on the things I hated to do. So, we were a good pair and complemented each other's weaker areas. But there was one thing I noticed: she really had a hard time apologizing for her mistakes.

Sacred Value: Apologies are foundational in relationships. If you don't apologize, it's because you are elevating your comfort over another person's pain.

Identity: My identity tells me to center on grace. There is something she needs to work through, so in the beginning I just chalked it up to wagon issues. After all, admitting mistakes and apologizing for them can be difficult for any of us.

I first noticed her propensity to avoid apologizing the first time she went on parent leave, and I was running a zoom training she set up before she left. When I started the meeting, I couldn't get in and, within a minute, the client called, complaining that her staff couldn't get into the zoom meeting because the link was wrong. I scurried to address the problem. I created a new link, sent it to the client, the staff got it, and all parties soon joined the link. This happened several more times when my colleague was away. It was the weirdest thing that every single time she would leave, something like this would happen.

When I shared with her that it happened, her response was always something to the effect of, "Glad you were able to get it handled," or "I was just moving so quickly trying to wrap things up before I left." Never an apology or an acknowledgement of the position that her mistake put me in. It started to bother me. But not in a sitting-in-the-pit-of-my-stomach kind of way, but the feeling of a mosquito in your tent kind of way. It's bothersome but not devastating.

Fast forward months later. We had a client that was composed primarily of people of color. The team that we worked directly with were all Black folks with the exception of 2-3 people.

Sacred Value: I have strong values about showing up for BIPOC (especially Black) folks who are on the frontlines of DEI. They have a lot of pressure to prove their decisions, and actions as worthy and successful. I wasn't going to let them down.

Identity: As a Black woman, I feel it is my *duty* to show up for other BIPOC folks and do what I can to make them, and me, shine.

In spaces like these, my colleague was brilliant. She didn't take up a lot of space, she asked perfect questions that I didn't think of, and just navigated well despite being the only white person in the space most of the time.

But one day, the client reached out to me (as the primary contractor) and shared some feedback they had gotten about my colleague.

My colleague and I had been facilitating a meeting with this client. My colleague said something that came across completely different from what she was actually trying to convey. I had been multitasking in the chat and only caught the tail end of her input. Sure, it sounded "off" to me, but I was 100% confident with her racial analysis and just figured since I didn't hear the entire statement, I missed the point.

Sure enough, others heard what she said as very racially offensive. When my colleague explained to me what she was trying to say, it made perfect sense. But, by this time, not only were they incensed by the interaction in the meeting, but they also brought up other situations that concerned them about her--some of which I had observed myself and had already spoken to her about. The client then requested that she not attend a very important upcoming meeting because of these concerns. She could still participate in the smaller team meetings but not the next big one. To make things worse, it was the last meeting of the year, so there was no organic opportunity for my colleague to make things clear.

I know many can't relate to this, but many Black folks will: you never ever want to be the Black woman who brings the problematic white woman to the party. And this is exactly how I was feeling. But the cognitive dissonance was alive and real. On one hand, this person was my friend and would never do anything to harm me or our business. On the other hand, as a Black woman, I had to believe the experiences of my people of color.

Sacred Value: I have sacred values about not putting Black folks in a position where they had to justify their reality or truth. Since I experienced this so often, I know what that feels like to not be believed, and will not do that to another Black person.

Identity: My identity as a consultant is framed in elevating voices of color. It's who I am. At the same time, my platform is grace. In

130

this situation, how do I elevate the voices or Black folks while extending grace to my friend? It was, after all, a mistake. The next day, I shared the client's feedback with my colleague. She cried.

Sacred Value: I have a sacred value of making space for people's humanity. Many people believe that white women shouldn't cry or emote on Black women and women of color. That's not my belief in general.

Identity: If I am about grace and humanity, I must make room for the human experience. Crying is part of that experience. Most of the time, I can tell the difference between manipulative tears and tears of shame or frustration.

She asked me questions about who said what and wanted to know how I interpreted what she said. To that question, I had to give an honest response and say I wasn't fully listening. But what I did hear matched the reaction we got from the client.

Here is where I went wrong. What I should have done is told her *everything* they said. It wasn't pretty. But in the interest of sparing her feelings, I withheld details. The story began to unravel and become disjointed as I tried to cut and paste, leaving out parts here and there. I imagine that it appeared to her that I was either covering something up or lying — which I was. This of course made her more upset.

I tried to soothe her. "I know it was a mistake. Next time it could be me. I'm sorry you had to go through this. It sucks." I apologized for not telling her the entire truth, which must have left her with more questions, confusion, and likely distrust of me.

The next day we spoke again, but this time, I expressed my frustration that after supporting her and listening to her the day before, I felt that she didn't see the position that I was placed in as her partner and as a Black woman. Even though it was a mistake, there was a lot of blowback on me. My name was on the contract. My reputation was on the line. I told her I was frustrated that she hadn't even asked if I was ok, or how I felt, or what I needed — all of which I asked her.

Her first words after me sharing this with her were, "I'm torn."

I took a deep breath as I remembered how she taught her white clients and allies to respond in similar situations. She teaches that, when a person of color says, "Ouch," you respond to that concern.

You don't say, "I'm torn."

I'm torn?

"I'm torn," she said.

She went on to say, "I want to honor your truth, but I just see it differently."

My first thought was *what does my truth have to do with your perception?* What I heard her saying was, "I am choosing to center myself regardless of what I am trained to do. Regardless of how you feel. I'm torn because what I feel is more important than how you were impacted or what you need. I'm torn because I don't believe what you are saying."

I immediately ended the zoom call before I said something not so gracious. The next day I told her that I'd like to continue to work on our existing clients, but I did not want to move forward with new clients.

Sacred Value: I have strong values about being seen. It is an essential value for me to share space (personal, professional, spiritual, mental etc.) with people who see me. I'm clear she was unwilling or unable to see me.

Identity: I am all about cutting ties early and moving on. This is how I have survived and protected myself. My last exchange with her was charged because my interpretation was that "I'm not worth her discomfort of acknowledging how her mistake has impacted me." Even months later.

At some point after this, she did finally say, "Hey, I hear you, and I'm going to work on my shit about not apologizing". This still wasn't an apology. This is when I knew that I'd never get the apology I felt I deserved. I was done.

As weeks went on after our separation, I kept feeling a lingering, nagging feeling that was really bothering me. I couldn't put my finger on it, but it was there. I talked to my therapist and my sister circle. They clearly understood how I felt and were supportive, but still, that didn't take away this weird feeling that I couldn't name and couldn't shake. Then it finally hit me like a ton of bricks.

I was angry at **myself.** For months, I was all but begging this white woman to apologize to me. I *needed* her to see me. To understand me. The fact that she refused only dug the knife in deeper. The knife that *I* was holding by the way. Not her. This made me furious with myself. I vowed after many negative experiences with white women to never put myself in a position where their actions affected me or where my value was in any way tied to their opinions or perspectives. Why did I trust her? After all, she was doing what white women do, right?

Enter grace.

I had to be real with myself that she wasn't just a "white woman." She was my *friend*. And there it was, folks. Racism urges us to compartmentalize and label our pain so that we can protect ourselves. If she were just a white woman then this all made sense, and I didn't have to look any deeper. But if she was my friend, I am obligated to process my emotions, confront my own complicity in this, and figure things out.

If we are really going to do this *grace* thing, we can no longer say, "Oh, this white woman snubbed me at the check-out counter – she's probably racist." She may be, but we can't default to that, even though it's easier and safer to do. Maybe her husband is having an affair with a woman who looks just like me. Who knows?

So here is my model for **Grace in Conflict:**

Gather yourself/Get some space – Often our immediate reaction is going to be our hardwired response, which is typically more fear-based than grace-based. It took me a few weeks until I figured it out in the shower. I had to untangle myself completely before I could see things clear eyed.

Reflect on your part - I had to come to terms with all of the ways that I was complicit in this process. I had to admit that I didn't communicate that clearly because I wasn't telling her the whole truth about what they said. This added to her confusion and frustration.

I had to name and respect all the emotions that were running through my mind and heart. I was angry at myself but leveled it at her. I was hurt that she just didn't apologize. I was embarrassed about how my Black clients saw me. I felt guilty that I didn't catch what she said because I would have called it out immediately.

Ask what-if questions – This is the part where you have to walk in their shoes. Imagine what they could have possibly been experiencing. The way to access that is by asking what-if questions.

- We both had wagon issues. She happens to be white, and I happen to be Black. But what if these differences had nothing to do with her reactions?
- What if she was hurt because she felt like I took our client's side over hers?
- What if she was trying to talk to me, but I was too angry to hear her? After all, we did delay three scheduled attempts to talk. By the time we did, perhaps both of us were too "over it" to go there.
- What if she was embarrassed that she created a mess all because of an accident?
- What if I had thought a little while longer and came up with a truthful but measured way to break the news to her about the client feedback?

Create an intention - what do you want and why – This is super important because depending on who the conflict is with, you'll need to know what outcomes we want. Sometimes, we want to distance ourselves from that person, sometimes it's a coworker that we have to see every day. Sometimes it's your biggest client and you have to make the choice between your peace and the income. Whatever it is, it's important to set an intention, and act from that. I always missed this step. I always only wanted one thing. **To make the awkwardness stop and make everyone feel ok**. Even if it means lying to them or myself.

With my colleague, I never deliberately created space for that intended outcome. Things were just left hanging out there and it still is. It's no wonder that this is the last chapter that I am writing. Because I knew that if I wrote about it, I would have to honor my own words. So, here is my intention, I am going to give myself a couple more months and if she doesn't reach out, I will. I intend on us both being in a better place to hear one another. I intend on both of us being whole.

Exhale – you've stepped back and reflected, you stepped out of yourself and put yourself in their shoes. You've done the work to look deeply at what you want the outcome to be and now – exhale and let it go. Trust that your higher power will take it from here. Don't mentally micromanage. Just let it go.

Having gone through these steps, I can say that I don't feel any negativity or bitterness toward my colleague. At this point, I'm just dealing with the residual gunk that is always there to remind me that people aren't safe, I'm not good enough, blah blah... the usual wagon stuff.

Organizations

I work with organizational leaders to find a way to innovatively manage conflict in a transformative way that moves us away from a reactive or punitive model to a proactive/restorative model where people are encouraged to self-reflect, collaborate on solutions, and work in harmony.

I still use the GRACE model with leaders with some slight changes:

- Gather yourself/your leadership team
- Reflect on your complicity as individuals and as a leadership body as it relates to the current organizational state
- Ask the "what if" questions
- Create an organizational intention as a team
- Establish goals, execute, and evaluate, repeat

What is Restorative Justice?

"Restorative Justice" describes a dialogue process of resolving conflict. Originally used in the criminal justice system, it related to severe crimes, and provided a platform for victims and offenders to engage in dialogue that promoted forgiveness, redemption, and healing.

What is Restorative Justice?

As Restorative Justice evolved, more and more organizations began to realize that they can use Restorative Justice Principles in their daily work to build, maintain and repair relationships. With this change in objective came a change in terminology - **Restorative Culture**. Many organizations have worked to embrace the philosophy of a restorative culture as a means to address conflict, team-build, and encourage honest dialogue aimed at creating a greater sense of community and safety.

Restorative Justice: Framing Conflict through a Lens of Grace

PUNITIVE APPROACH	RESTORATIVE APPROACH
Zooms in on specific conflict	Zooms out to contextualize conflict within the organizational culture
Focuses on impact of the organization	Focuses on impact of the people
Establishes guilt and consequences	Establishes accountability and restoration

Whether we are talking about individual conflict or organizational conflict, it is work that must begin long before the actual conflict erupts.

Grace equity is the solution and is implemented by role-playing and discussing scenarios so people are not caught off-guard. And it is done by introducing the concept of grace to conflict so that the best runway is laid for resolution, making it far easier to navigate the choppy waters of human conflict.

CHAPTER 11 – WE'RE ALL SWIMMERS

"A person with ubuntu is open and available to others, affirming of others, does not feel threatened that others are able and good, for he or she has a proper self-assurance that comes from knowing that he or she belongs in a greater whole and is diminished when others are humiliated or diminished, when others are tortured or oppressed."

— *Desmond Tutu*

I saved one important "C" for now because everything we have discussed prior to this point rests on our abilities of **communication.** Grace work is practice — trial and error. I believe that access to any meaningful conversation rests on the foundation of grace. The framework for talking about race is one where compassion meets accountability, and there is deep acceptance that we are at different places in our understanding, perceptions, and capacity to honestly talk about race and racism.

Let me explain with a story. There are two morals within this story. I hope you will catch them both.

I learned to swim in my twenties. Because there weren't enough registrations for the youth swim class or the adult swim class separately, the organizers lumped us all in one session together. So, there I was at twenty-something, alongside eight- and nine-year-olds, learning to swim. Talk about a crash course in humiliation and humility. I got a front row seat to kids who were Michael-Phelpsing past me at speeds that deserved a moving violation as I splashed, and doggie paddled my way across the pool.

But one thing was for sure. *We were all swimmers.* There were some who learned quicker, some who learned more slowly, older folks, younger folks, folks of different genders, ethnicities, lived experiences and backgrounds, but for sure, we were all swimmers. At no point were we pitted against each other. Yes, we could clearly see who the better swimmers were. But the culture of the class was clear: if you are in the pool, you are considered a swimmer.

One of the requirements to pass the class was to jump off the diving board — the low-dive. But I was terrified to do it. A line of children formed behind me, itching for their chance to walk to the edge of the diving board and make the plunge. But they were all delayed by me — a grown ass woman, gripped with fear, behaving as if she was jumping into the Grand Canyon - sans parachute!

After some time, it was clear that I did not have the courage to make the leap. But rather than taunt me — a skill in which eight-year-olds hold advanced degrees — they began to cheer me on. "You can do it", yelled one child. Another child encouraged, "don't be a-scared." This fueled me, partly because my ego wouldn't allow me to continue to look like a chicken, but mostly because I knew whether I belly-flopped or did a swan dive, they would be just as excited. In retrospect, I remember how good it felt to feel like I couldn't lose. Just taking the risk was the victory. We shared a common goal. We were all swimmers. That's it. That's all.

Just like we all willingly signed up for that swim class, sometimes a group of us come together to have conversations about race. When this happens, we must remember that we are all swimmers in the cesspool that is racism. Some of us are drowning in the oppression, some are backstroking our way to the side of the pool to hold on for dear life, some or gliding through with the privilege of swim fins, goggles, and other equipment to enhance their swim experience. But we came together to learn how to be better swimmers. We didn't make the person who had the swim fins and goggles feel bad about having them. We didn't tell the people who were backstroking that they were doing it wrong. And we absolutely speed swam to the aid of those drowning. All of these occurred without judgment, shame, or one-upmanship.

When we were learning how to swim, we understood that we would all be learning and integrating concepts at different paces. It was a given that some would be better than others. Nobody cared.

But in terms of coming together to dialogue about race and racism there is no space and grace for being a learner. There isn't a spectrum or guide that indicates where you are in your fluency of race and racism. We don't have a mechanism to perhaps say, "oh, you are at level 4 in your racial analysis. "You can do it." "Don't be a-scared." "Here are the mistakes I made when I was at level 4." We falsely set up two extremes. Either you are an outright racist, or you're not. Either you are Michael Phelps, or you are the ass who goes around pulling people's swim trunks down beneath the water. There's no in-between in the game or race dialogue when there should be a continuum.

Moral #1

We often forget that we are all heirs of a devastatingly bad system. Victim or oppressor, these awful mindsets were not naturally present in any of us at birth; we had to be taught through precept or osmosis to think the way we did. Said another way, we are all trying to work it out, and we are at different places in the journey.

We have not figured out how to navigate the *messy middle* where most of us live. None of us are the most oppressed there has ever been in an organizational setting, and none of us are the worst perpetrators.

How do we process the messy middle — the purgatory designed for people like you and me who are at different points of learning, analysis, and understanding? We'll get to the answer in a moment.

The second part to this story involved a man I met on the first day of swim class. This man came to sit next to me as I sat on the edge of the pool and dangled my legs in the water. My nerves were doing cartwheels inside knowing that, soon, I would be pushing myself far outside of my boundaries. I was afraid of swimming but determined to face this fear.

This man had the air of a macho-guy. He was physically buff and talked with a thick New York City accent. He neatly fit the description of what I had always thought of as the veritable tough guy. But there was one thing about him that completely threw me: wrapped around his rippling biceps were bright yellow floaties that little kids wore when they swam to keep them above water.

He must have noticed me checking out this odd addition to his swimwear because he chuckled and said, "Can't be too careful. Am I right?"

I didn't laugh out loud, but on the inside? I was hysterically belly laughing. I was rolling on my tummy pounding my hand against the ground laughing. Yet, at the same time, there was something sweet and endearing about his "I don't give a shit" authenticity that made me think, "I know that's right. Do you, boo."

I watched as he hopped into the pool and swam around, competing with the kids, and having fun. He was noisy and a bit annoying, but he was a part of the class, and I had heard the instructor's message loud and clear: we are all swimmers.

After our third or fourth class, we were all climbing out of the pool. He walked ahead of me toward the locker rooms. Just before he made the turn toward the men's locker room, I heard him faintly comment in the distance...

"I took this class because my brother drowned when I was a kid and I'm just tired of feeling sad and shit..."

It was revealed that he had signed up for the class after years of grieving the drowning death of his younger brother. He never went near a pool or a beach, creek, river, or any body of water for that matter. The pain of the loss had grown so unbearable that he felt one way to confront his pain head-on was to learn to swim and take his power back.

He shifted from this arrogant, noisy, silly man to a sensitive, vulnerable, courageous big brother grieving the deepest loss. He was actively working his way back to something resembling wholeness. I had been blessed to witness another human being facing his fears with that all-important mix of courage and trepidation as he sought his breakthrough.

In that moment, he was a different man. He changed right before my eyes, and I changed before his — whether he noticed it or not. I knew his story now, so I was forever connected to him. So connected, I am now connecting you to him as well.

I listened to his story and heard his heart, so he was forever a part of my story. He was human again — not a cartoon caricature. He was relatable. I could see myself in his trauma. My younger sister and I are best friends. We refer to each other as soulmates. I was incredibly empathetic to his pain born out of the love he had for his

143

brother, the searing pain of watching the boy die, and the fight to take back his own life as best he could.

Moral #2

Knowing someone's story changes you, and it changes them. In this man, I found compassion, love, grace and courage in a new way. It has been decades, and I still talk about him. I believe that, deep down, this is why I use myself and my stories as examples in my training and interactions. People can see themselves better if you share yourself, as opposed to teaching them concepts about how to share themselves.

This is one of the best examples of grace equity I can share because it shows how grace calms, it illuminates the humanity of another such that there is no distance between two hearts. There is only sameness. We are one. We are all swimmers — we are all humans.

Grace equity says:
- You are allowed to be you.
- You are empowered to grow at your pace.
- You are ok.
- You can be uncomfortable in the process of moving forward.
- You can rest in your own skin and not try to impress others.
- You are safe to make your emotions accessible.

This is a paradigm of curvature, levity, openness, responsiveness, agility, and connectivity as we reach out for each other and stay connected. To borrow from the swimming analogy, we don't allow each other to drown in the deep waters of racism. We jump in and teach others to swim. We help everyone keep their heads above water.

Grace equity writes a certified check to all who will embrace it — that they will be seen, heard, valued, honored, respected, and never alone as they move through the process. It is where wholeness meets the work of anti-racism. Where you can be your whole self and reveal the real you.

Everyone has a story. And knowing the stories of others will impact and shift the way you see them. The kind of low-resolution thinking people resort to in organizations are the categories that make it easy to sort the world around us. We just call people by the category we think they best fit into: Black person, female person, married person, etc. But the stories behind each label add color, dimension, and complexity to your understanding of who they are and how they behave. Suddenly, their quirks and habits, their decisions, their mindsets are not just points of contention or confusion; they naturally follow from the experiences that helped to shape them.

Grace is like the magic goggles that allow us to see behind the façade people display each day into the deeper places that reveal them more honestly and allows us to connect with them more fully.

In 2009, 20th Century Fox released the blockbuster movie, Avatar (Cameron, 2009) about a space age contingent who travel to a distant planet to recover an energy source. But, in order to get access to this energy, they must displace the native living there. These natives are known as the Na'vi.

The Na'vi share a special greeting — "oel ngati kameie" which translates, "I see you." Imagine what life would be like if, instead of meaningless greetings like "How ya, doin" or "Workin' hard or hardly working," we could say something as meaningful as "I see you?"

Is that not what each of us wants: to be seen? Not in the self-aggrandizing, prideful way that calls attention to oneself. But in the humbling way we call on the universe to acknowledge that we are here. We exist. We matter.

So how do we navigate the messy middle? *We see each other.* In my swim class, there was no messy middle because we all saw each other as swimmers. Swimmers who learned differently, swimmers with different backgrounds, swimmers with different reasons for being there, or even swimmers in the making.

In discussions of race, there is no such common baseline for us to connect. The only thing that I've ever known to get us even close to seeing each other with such complete wholeness is grace.

May we all be swimmers...in grace.

WORKS CITED

Asare, J. G. (2022, July). *Dear Sesame Place: Here Are Three Ways To Actually Address Racist Practices*. Retrieved from www.forbes.com: https://www.forbes.com/sites/janicegassam/2022/07/21/dear-sesame-place-here-are-three-ways-to-address-racist-practices/?sh=6568b8707ead

Bayne, B. C. (2022, February). *How 'woke' became the least woke word in U.S. English*. Retrieved from Washingtonpost.com: https://www.washingtonpost.com/opinions/2022/02/02/black-history-woke-appropriation-misuse/

Cameron, J. (Director). (2009). *Avataar* [Motion Picture].

CBS News Philadelphia. (2022, July). *More Families Come Forward With Complaints After Sesame Place Character Allegedly Ignores 2 Young Black Girls, Attorney Says*. Retrieved from www.cbsnews.com: https://www.cbsnews.com/philadelphia/news/more-families-complaint-sesame-place-character-ignores-black-girls/

Chartered Institute of Personnel and Development . (2022). *How to talk about race at work*. London: Royal Charter.

Clark, M., Robertson, M., & Young, S. (2019). I feel your pain: A critical review of organizational research on empathy. *Journal of Organizational Behavior*, 166-192.

Facing History and Ourselves. (2010, June 15). *TRC-Victims Confronting Perpetrator*. Retrieved from Youtube: https://www.youtube.com/watch?v=Tw5aTObdO5Y

Jodi. (2022, July 16). Retrieved from Instagram: https://www.instagram.com/p/CgGAHtyFoHg/

Lanzoni, S. (2015, October). *The Atlantic*. Retrieved from www.atlantic.com: https://www.theatlantic.com/health/archive/2015/10/a-short-history-of-empathy/409912/

NBC Philadelphia News. (2022, July). *'Racist Act': New Video Surfaces in Sesame Place Controversy*. Retrieved from NBCphiladelphia.com: https://www.nbcphiladelphia.com/news/local/new-video-surfaces-in-sesame-place-controversy/3313893/

NotInMyColour. (2022, Jan). *NotinMyColor*. Retrieved from Twitter: https://twitter.com/NotInMyColour/status/1482437672706531328

Sesame Place. (2022, July 17). *sesameplace*. Retrieved from Instagram: https://www.instagram.com/p/CgInXl6uy4T/

Sesame Place. (2022, July). *sesameplace*. Retrieved from Instagram: https://www.instagram.com/p/CgLBV9mOC0q/

Western States Center. (2001). *Assessing Organizational Racism.* Retrieved from https://drive.google.com/file/d/1iki01-yjMkTdG2b7augsRksU6ovtkHn3/view

Wikipedia. (2022, October). *List of truth and reconciliation commissions*. Retrieved from Wikipedia: https://en.wikipedia.org/wiki/List_of_truth_and_reconciliation_commissions

ABOUT THE AUTHOR

Dr. Michelle Majors is the author of Trust the Process: Reflections of a Nonprofit Race Equity Movement, and Grace Equity: Reimagining Conversations about Equity in the Workplace. A Seattle native, she earned her Masters in Transformational Leadership and her Doctorate in Educational Leadership—both from Seattle University.

Dr. Majors is a Race Equity Consultant by day and a world class professional introvert at night, so you will likely find her playing catch with her two German Shepherds, Tommi and Ghost, binge watching her favorite show, Ted Lasso for the one-millionth time, and more than likely listening to Jill Scott in the background. You can visit her online at www.GraceEquity.com.

If you enjoyed this book, please help others find it by leaving a review on the site where you found it. Reviews are the best way to tell the website to share this message with others. Thank you for your support!

Dr. Michelle Majors

Made in United States
Troutdale, OR
06/25/2024

20808338R00096